Alba Belegu

Knowledge Transfer and Learning

D1807002

Alba Belegu

Knowledge Transfer and Learning

Knowledge transfer and learning in and between projects

LAP LAMBERT Academic Publishing

Impressum/Imprint (nur für Deutschland/ only for Germany)
Bibliografische Information der Deutschen Nationalbibliothek: Die Deutsche Nationalbibliothek
verzeichnet diese Publikation in der Deutschen Nationalbibliografie; detaillierte bibliografische
Daten sind im Internet über http://dnb.d-nb.de abrufbar.
 Alle in diesem Buch genannten Marken und Produktnamen unterliegen warenzeichen-, marken-
oder patentrechtlichem Schutz bzw. sind Warenzeichen oder eingetragene Warenzeichen der
jeweiligen Inhaber. Die Wiedergabe von Marken, Produktnamen, Gebrauchsnamen,
Handelsnamen, Warenbezeichnungen u.s.w. in diesem Werk berechtigt auch ohne besondere
Kennzeichnung nicht zu der Annahme, dass solche Namen im Sinne der Warenzeichen- und
Markenschutzgesetzgebung als frei zu betrachten wären und daher von jedermann benutzt
werden dürften.

Coverbild: www.ingimage.com

Verlag: LAP LAMBERT Academic Publishing AG & Co. KG
Dudweiler Landstr. 99, 66123 Saarbrücken, Deutschland
Telefon +49 681 3720-310, Telefax +49 681 3720-3109
Email: info@lap-publishing.com

Herstellung in Deutschland:
Schaltungsdienst Lange o.H.G., Berlin
Books on Demand GmbH, Norderstedt
Reha GmbH, Saarbrücken
Amazon Distribution GmbH, Leipzig
ISBN: 978-3-8383-9707-8

Imprint (only for USA, GB)
Bibliographic information published by the Deutsche Nationalbibliothek: The Deutsche
Nationalbibliothek lists this publication in the Deutsche Nationalbibliografie; detailed
bibliographic data are available in the Internet at http://dnb.d-nb.de.
 Any brand names and product names mentioned in this book are subject to trademark, brand
or patent protection and are trademarks or registered trademarks of their respective holders.
The use of brand names, product names, common names, trade names, product descriptions
etc. even without a particular marking in this works is in no way to be construed to mean that
such names may be regarded as unrestricted in respect of trademark and brand protection
legislation and could thus be used by anyone.

Cover image: www.ingimage.com

Publisher: LAP LAMBERT Academic Publishing AG & Co. KG
Dudweiler Landstr. 99, 66123 Saarbrücken, Germany
Phone +49 681 3720-310, Fax +49 681 3720-3109
Email: info@lap-publishing.com

Printed in the U.S.A.
Printed in the U.K. by (see last page)
ISBN: 978-3-8383-9707-8

Acknowledgement

Firstly, I owe my gratitude to my supervisor, Professor Ralf Müller, for his continuous support, guidance and advice throughout the research and writing of the thesis. Without his support the result would have not been the same. I would also like to thank sincerely the company located in UK which gave me this exceptional opportunity to do the research in their premises, with full financial support provided by them for travel and accommodation. Being present in Company X during my one month stay in UK was one in a lifetime opportunity and has opened many doors for me. I am sincerely in debt to the kindness of the interviewees who allocated their scarce time to provide inputs to the research questions. I am grateful to my fellow colleagues for their moral support throughout the thesis and the whole master programme. They will sincerely be missed. A special thanks to the Erasmus Mundus programme, without which this study and my entire Master experience wouldn't have been possible. And last, but not least a special thank you to my family, loved ones and friends for being there for me. My family have taught me the values of good education, and have given me inspiration to be like them through persistence, hard work and strong personality.

Umeå , January 2009

TABLE OF CONTENTS

LIST OF TABLES

LIST OF FIGURES

ACRONYMS AND ABBREVIATIONS

APM	Association of Project Management
ATM	Air Traffic Management
CBT	Computer Based Training
CDOX	Career Development Opportunity Exchange
CMM	Capability Maturity Model
CPR	Critical Project Review
EC	European Commission
ICT	Information & Communication Technology
KPI	Key Performance Indicator
LLRC	Lessons Learned Review Committee
MPA	Major Projects Association
MRI	Master Record Index
MSPME	Master in Strategic Project Management European
OJT	On Job Training
PDFO	Programme Development & Finance Office
PgM	Programme Manager
PM	Project Manager
PMA	Project Management Association
PMBOK	Project Management Body of Knowledge
PMI	Project Management Institute
PMO	Project Management Office
PMP	Project Management Plan
PNS	Project Network Structure
PP	Project Planner
QM	Quality Manager
RAMP	Risk Analysis & Management Process
SPM	Senior Programme Manager
UK	United Kingdom

The acronyms used for the programmes and projects of Case Company X have not been mentioned for security reasons

1.   INTRODUCTION

1.1   Background

Nowadays, organizations are faced with a complex and continuous changing environment. In order to solve tasks and be successful, the project-based way of working is adopted, which is considered more flexible and innovative (Brady, Marshall, Prencipe & Tell, 2003; Hobday, 2000). Projects have flexibility and fluidity in them, which is a requirement for adapting to the pace of changing circumstances. Moreover, projects are considered as creative entities, generating and applying new knowledge, which undoubtedly can be transferred and shared in and between projects and in a company wide context.

Except general knowledge in the field of project management and its extensive usage, researchers believe that the prior experience of the project professionals or project based companies is crucial, as well as their behavior (APM, 2006, p.114). In addition, the importance of organizational learning and knowledge management has been increased throughout the years, as shown by the substantial amount of research conducted in this area (Cooper, Lynesis & Bryant, 2002; Keegan and Turner, 2001; Williams, 2003). Accordingly, there has been an increasing interest in the possibilities of cross fertilization of knowledge and practice in and between projects. Researchers stress continuously the importance of being able to learn from previous experiences and share this knowledge in and between projects, in order to avoid repetition of mistakes and redundancy of information (Prencipe & Tell, 2001). Davies & Hobday (2005) also emphasize the importance of inter and intra-project learning in achieving competitive success. Having the ability to create knowledge and conduct project learning is considered crucial to the long term market success and a capability for gaining competitive advantage (Ayas, 1997; Prencipe et al., 2001; Williams, 2003). Nonaka & Takeuchi (1995) present an influential part of this research, and elaborate it in details.

Project based companies are advised to develop various learning mechanisms which enhance the accumulation and transfer of relevant knowledge (Brady & Davies, 2004). Nevertheless, even though the importance of knowledge transfer and project learning is increasingly important for companies, only few companies have institutionalized the practices (i.e. mechanisms and processes) to capture and disseminate the knowledge into subsequent projects (Schindler & Eppler, 2003). Moreover, very few studies have established the effectiveness of the mechanisms and processes for knowledge transfer and learning in and between projects. There is the possibility of some learning mechanisms and processes being appropriate for managing and transferring the knowledge accumulated in and between projects, and others not being the appropriate channels. If the appropriate mechanisms are overlooked, the opportunity to enhance future project performance is missed, as well as the opportunity to avoid repetition of same mistakes. Cooper et al., (2002) advocates that knowledge created is often lost when the project is finished. It represents a cost for the company to repeat the mistakes and utilize ineffective mechanisms and processes. Moreover, the mechanisms and processes for knowledge transfer should be economically feasible. Cooper et al., (2002, p.213) observe that *"We have yet to discern how to systematically extract and disseminate management lessons as we move from project to project."*

The researcher of this study has tried to apply the models and propositions proposed by the literature on Case Company X where the research was conducted. In order for the researcher to provide recommendations on how to increase knowledge transfer and improve learning, only one model and proposition was not applicable. There was a need represented to combine a few models and propositions. Therefore, in order to understand how a practitioner can increase knowledge transfer and improve learning in and between projects, a qualitative case study at Company X in UK was made by the researcher. The research question is described below in the text.

1.2   Choice of Subject

When the researcher conducted this study, she was a student attending Master of Science in Strategic Project Management European (MSPME) programme, with a consortium of three universities: Heriot-Watt University in Scotland, Politecnico di Milano in Italy and Umeå School of Business in Sweden. Considering that the researcher's master is in Project Management, she decided to apply the gained knowledge in her thesis, with special interest in knowledge transfer and learning in and between projects in companies.

The researcher chose the topic for three reasons:
- It was mutually agreed as a topic by the company wherein the research was conducted and the researcher;
- A wide variety of project management literature indicates the importance of knowledge management and learning in project based companies; and
- The researcher has a special interest in the research in knowledge management and learning.

Company X has initiated the idea of dissertation topic to be conducted by a MSPME student. The benefit was mutual, considering that the data was provided for the researcher, and the researcher produced a final report containing the findings and recommendations which would be used by Case Company X. Case Company X has provided the information and has channeled the researcher to the right people to be interviewed.

1.2.1 Company overview

Case Company X provides X services. Case Company X is a leader in the industry in terms of technological and business development and also sells a range of products and consultancy services. Safety is Case Company X's first and foremost priority but they also aim to provide their service in an efficient and cost-effective way.

The company is the market leader in UK, and employees and top management of the company expressed that the company was reasonably competent in accomplishing projects. *The name of the programmes and projects, as well as of the company will not be disclosed for security reasons.*

1.2.2 Project Management Application in Case Company X

During these years Company X employees have developed a wide-ranging expertise in project and programme management. Since it became partly privatized, it transformed from a functional to a matrix organization. Case Company X can be considered as a well integrated project based company, in which strong interrelationships between its projects and its corporate strategies are visible. Projects are primary business mechanisms, which provide an arena for coordinating all the business functions of Case Company X. Projects contain a range of technical and functional disciplines, therefore, demanding a range of specialized knowledge inputs. For each project, a Project Manager (PM) and a project team are appointed.

The company is now organized as a matrix with development departments on one axis and projects on the other. The company is organized around divisions focused on six specific programmes, which incorporate many projects. Functional disciplines like finance, human resources and safety are matrixed. In a matrix structure individuals stay within their functional departments while performing work on one or more projects. Nevertheless, people report to both functional heads and project managers.

Autonomy requirement of the project team has been able to be kept, while at the same time they were embedded with company policies, which integrate project activities within company routines. Case Company X has created a complex inter-dependent system between projects and stakeholders, which system has the ability to adapt to changing circumstances. Moreover, this resulted in increased knowledge diffusion, and new work practice emerging. Case Company X has managed the fusion of governance and engineering in project management, which is usually considered a challenge in the research world.

Recently, Case Company X has initiated several steps to promote knowledge transfer and learning because they realized that the company would benefit if various project knowledge transfer and learning mechanisms and processes were applied by project and programme managers. The goal was that every project manager gets a broader project management repertoire and knowledge by taking advantages of 'lessons learned'. Furthermore, project managers would improve in illustration on each other's experience and seeking advice and feedback when a problem arises.

1.3   Research Objectives

The prime objective of the research is to identify and analyze how Case Company X manages and transfers Project Management Knowledge and promotes learning.

The prime research objective has been broken down into three minor objectives: The three research sub-objectives are:

(i)   To identify the different types of project-learning mechanisms and processes used by Case Company X to transfer effectively the accumulated knowledge in and between projects.

(ii)   To identify and examine the type of company environment established by Case Company X, to promote, support and enhance learning in and between projects.

(iii)   To identify and examine the role of individual project professionals in effective knowledge transfer and learning in and between projects, as well as the incentives provided to share knowledge.

1.4   Research Question

To achieve the objectives, one research question was defined:

"How can knowledge transfer be increased and learning improved in and between projects at Company X in UK?"

In a learning perspective, projects need to be viewed in terms of their relationship with ongoing activities, norms and practices operating in the rest of the company. However, even though existing studies note the importance of such company factors, the unit of analysis in the research conducted is the project itself.

The case study is done with the purpose of helping Case Company X perform better in the project level, specifically facilitating knowledge transfer and learning in and between projects. Furthermore, the study is expected to increase and contribute to the awareness of Case Company X, towards the benefits of facilitating knowledge transfer and learning.

1.5   Definitions and Concepts

Definitions of the main concepts that are used in the study are provided. Nevertheless, during the analysis of the articles in project management, the researcher was faced with the term "knowledge management" and "project learning" expressed in different ways. As it has been stated by Leseure & Brookes (2004) project management and knowledge management can only go hand-in-hand. Furthermore, it is important to explain how the concepts are used and defined in the study.

1.5.1 Knowledge Management

In order to understand the categorization of knowledge, a brief understanding of knowledge management is provided.

The researcher of the study utilized the definition of knowledge of Mumford (1994):

"Knowledge is the acquisition of data or information. Sometimes it is not new knowledge but confirmation of past information".

Knowledge Management's role is to ensure that collective learning happens, and is facilitated through the most appropriate knowledge environment. In today's changing environment, knowledge is not static, but it needs to be identified, evaluated, acquired, transferred, stored, used, maintained and possibly disposed of (Drucker, 1993; Hamel, 2002; Nonaka, 1991; Pemberton & Stonehouse, 2000). Many management researchers consider it as competitive advantage (Drucker, 1993; Hamel, 2002; Nonaka, 1991; Pemberton et al., 2000). Organizations have resources which can be converted into capabilities, or can be retained as tacit knowledge. Knowledge management serves to collect and convert the individual knowledge into organizational knowledge (Bollinger & Smith, 2001; Pemberton et al., 2000; Spender, 1996). Furthermore, it can improve product development and quality, and establish a better relationship and understanding of customer and stakeholders (Davenport, Eccles & Prusak, 1992; Hauschild, Licht & Stein, 2001; Martensson, 2000; Skyrme, 1998). Large organizations pay more attention to the knowledge management, because it is more difficult to determine *"who knows what"* in these organizations (Davenport & Prusak, 1998, pp.58). An effective knowledge management strategy is important, considering that it facilitates and transfers knowledge, whilst reducing the time lost during research for a certain expertise.

1.5.2 Project based companies

The researcher uses the definition of project based companies of Hobday (2000):

"Project based companies are companies which organize a large portion of their operations and works as projects. They usually provide unique products and services".

The phenomenon of project based companies is increasing significantly in different industries, considering their flexibility and adaptability to the changing environment (Thiry & Deguire, 2007). The companies that run a large percentage of their business through projects are dependent on good project results. Furthermore, considering the impact that project results have on company results, rigid governance structures for projects and their management are necessary (Müller, 2009).

Governance entities exist at level of projects, programs and portfolios. The board of directors defines the portfolio goals, prioritization criteria and means for progress measure. Whereas, at project and program level, the sponsor or the steering groups decide on the deliverables as well as progress means and time (Müller, 2009).
Project based companies are a natural arena for knowledge management, because project management staff have continuous interaction and build upon tacit and explicit knowledge, during their movement within project phases, and also along different projects. Therefore, for project success we need the capturing of different categories of knowledge.

1.5.3 Project - based Learning

The researcher used the definition of a project from Turner & Müller (2003):

"A project is a temporary organization to which resources are assigned to undertake a unique, novel and transient endeavor managing the inherent uncertainty and need for integration in order to deliver beneficial objectives of change".

The researcher utilizes the definition of project learning from Ayas & Zenuik (2001):

"Project learning is defined as generation and acquisition of new knowledge and experience during the project execution".

Companies run projects ranging from unique to repetitive. When considering unique projects there are less opportunities for cumulative learning, because of the tasks not being repeated in the future (Brady et al., 2004). Nevertheless, in repetitive projects, learning from experience is possible considering that the tasks performed are repeated in many projects. Therefore, by reusing and recombining the knowledge, the organization can utilize knowledge assets more efficiently and take on more projects.

Kotnour (1999) argues that learning helps project managers to produce successful projects and to develop the adequate capabilities, like project management processes, as well as knowledge management processes. Furthermore, he states that at project level, project learning might be broken down into intra and inter-project learning, wherein knowledge is created and builds upon at individual and group level.

Intra- project learning takes place within the project, wherein project team members work on different tasks within the project. Moreover, it focuses mainly on successful delivery of a sole project. Inter-project learning takes place across different phases of the project, and it incorporates the capturing of new knowledge created and accumulated during project execution, as well as the transferring the knowledge to improve the performance of other projects (Prencipe et al., 2001; Schindler et al., 2003). It is also known as *'cross-project learning'* (DeFillippi & Arthur, 1998), *'project-to-project learning'* (Brady et al., 2004) or *'learning between projects'* (Keegan et al., 2001).

The new knowledge which is accumulated and stored with appropriate mechanisms and processes adds to the organizations knowledge base – organizational memory- and enhances the project performance. According to Nahapiet & Ghoshal (1998) organizational memory represents the intellectual capital, incorporating the knowledge and the capability to learn and develop the knowledge within an organization. Project learning incorporates the deliberate and systematic perceptions on project experience.

In the context of project environment, it is critical to create new knowledge, as well as systematically transfer it and apply it to modify operating routines, with the goal of enhancing project performance and effectiveness (Schindler et al., 2003). Accordingly, when companies identify and apply learning within projects it enables them *"to develop the company's capability to undertake current and future projects"* (APM, 2006, p.116). Learning and development involves the continual improvement of competencies in the company.

1.6   Research Purpose

Project Management literature has been extensively researching the topics in the field of "knowledge management "and "learning organization". The outcomes of the research done were findings on the mechanisms/methods and processes which enable knowledge creation and transfer and learning in projects and in company X. The researcher wanted to explore the up-to-date research done for mechanisms and processes in knowledge transfer and learning throughout a learning organization, and identifies the most appropriate and usable mechanisms and processes which are proposed by the literature. Moreover, the researcher wanted to compare the mechanisms proposed by literature with the mechanisms used by Case Company X for knowledge transfer and learning. And finally, the researcher wanted to understand the environment in which these mechanisms and processes co-exist.

The first purpose of the researcher is to answer the research question and achieve the research objectives. The theoretical base given in the literature review chapter will serve as a base to interpret the interviews and build a theory on as to how the knowledge context relates to the proposed scientific theory. The second purpose is to use the findings of this study to help Case Company X to treat learning and promote knowledge transfer in and between projects. Recommendation(s) produced for Case Company X will be based on the existing theoretical base as well as on the outcomes of the interpretation of the interviews.

1.7   Research Structure

In order to set the background for this study, the following chapters are developed

Chapter 1:   Introduction

Serves to provide general information about the research study.

Chapter 2:   Literature Review

Provides the theoretical background for the research, and introduces the terms used later in the analysis chapter. The literature is applied specifically to the research question; therefore emphasis is given on project knowledge transfer and learning mechanisms and processes. Moreover, the environment they co-exist in is elaborated.

Chapter 3:   Methodology

Introduces the research philosophy and the approach adopted in the research – the method used and the way the data is retrieved and analyzed. A qualitative case study is used, by collecting the data with semi-structured interviews tool.

Chapter 4:   Analysis of Data

Introduces the organized findings which are analyzed under the framework of a 'learning landscape', utilizing a Three-by-Three matrix. The account of the role of mechanisms and processes in knowledge transfer and learning is explored further through a detailed empirical analysis identifying the mechanisms at individual, project and organization level and the processes they are accompanied with. Moreover, the environment wherein these mechanisms and processes co-exist is analyzed. The data is collected from a company based in UK, who considers project management crucial for their business operations.

Chapter 5:   Discussion

Considering the big amount of data, they are presented in a more organized manner. Except for the brief summary of the data, some recommendations are introduced to mitigate the impact. The suggestions are presented according to the findings in the previous chapter.

Chapter 6:   Conclusion

The conclusion summarizes our findings and discussion points, and relates them to the research question and objectives to ensure our research has reached the objectives we expected. Limitations are also acknowledged and suggested future research is presented. Moreover, more detailed recommendations are also given. And a final positive comment concludes the research.

2. LITERATURE REVIEW

2.1 Overview on Project Knowledge Management

This chapter provides a review on the disciplines of project management and knowledge management. It is supported by reviewing the research articles in the field of project management, knowledge management and project-based learning. Articles illustrate the concepts of knowledge and learning from a project management's perspective. The articles are grouped based on three categories. Moreover, the company environment they co-exist in is elaborated further down. Analysis and review of the recent project management studies will be provided, by specifically analyzing different case studies wherein knowledge management in projects was applied. The outcome will be a basis for improved knowledge transfer and learning in and between projects.

Knowledge management concepts have challenged the project management orthodoxy – the traditional views of requirements for successful project management- represented by the Body of Knowledge (PMBOK, 2004). Knowledge management can take place differently in project management context. An appropriate knowledge management strategy needs to be applied, which creates a competitive advantage. Everyone in the project needs to work towards creating opportunities for knowledge creation (see Figure 1). The creation of knowledge is done through individual and company learning, achieved through socialization, embodying the knowledge through individual skills and work, and combining it into the technologies and other explicit expressions of knowledge commonly used within projects (Nonaka et al., 1995).

FIGURE 1

Knowledge Management Cycle

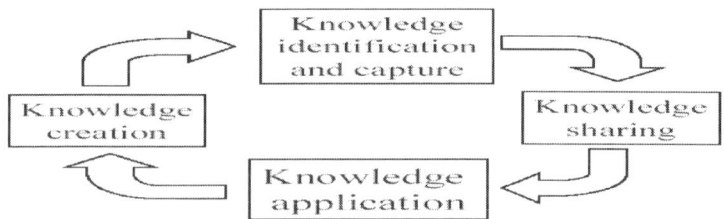

Source: Becerra-Fernandez,Gonzales & Sabherval, 2004,p.88

10

A categorization of the ways of improving learning and knowledge transfer in and between projects is provided, for the ease of understanding the different aspects of the study. There will be a total of three main categories: *Tacit and Explicit knowledge and Processes*. Furthermore, the environment these categories co-exist will be elaborated in more detail. According to Nonaka et al., (1995), knowledge can be divided into tacit and explicit knowledge. Other researchers also provide a similar approach to knowledge categorization. However, the researcher decided to elaborate on the category called processes, which are all the procedures followed for knowledge transfer and learning. This is to cover the concept and importance of the procedure behind knowledge transfer and learning. During the analysis of the articles, environment in which the knowledge transfer and learning is conducted seemed to play a crucial role. Therefore, a brief analysis of the environment and its role in knowledge transfer and learning in and between projects is provided.

A detailed emphasis of the articles underlining the specific categories of tacit and explicit knowledge as well as the processes is presented in Table 1, for the ease of understanding.

TABLE 1
CATEGORIZATION OF ARTICLES

Articles	Tacit	Explicit	Processes
Argyris, C. (1999)			✓
Ayas, K. (1996)	✓		
Cooper, Lynesis, Bryant (2000)		✓	
Hameri, Nihtilä (1998)		✓	✓
Harvey, Palmer, Speier (1998)		✓	
Karlsen, Gottschalk (2003)	✓		
Koskinen, Pihlanto, Vanharanta (2003)	✓	✓	✓
Kotnour, Tim (1999, 2000)	✓		
Mumford, Alan (1994)	✓		
Prencipe, Tell (2001)			✓
Schindler , Eppler (2003)	✓	✓	✓
Söderlund, Vaagaasar, Andersen (2008)		✓	✓
Woo, Clayton, Johnson, Flores, Ellis (2004)	✓	✓	
Zollo, Winter (2001)			✓

In tacit category, an importance is given to the mechanisms and processes that emphasize and show the *"soft"* ways of transferring knowledge between individual professionals.

Polanyi (1967) encapsulated the essence of tacit knowledge in the phrase *"We know more than we can tell"*. In tacit knowledge, researcher refers to the knowledge that is applied in and between people in projects. Tacit knowledge development is through experience, wherein learning is conducted and knowledge is gained. It is intangible and not easy to express, which makes it difficult to be articulated, formalized and most of all difficult to be transferred in and between projects. It is rooted deeply in an individual's actions and experience, as well as with the ideals, values, or emotions the individual embraces (Nonaka et al., 1995). Individuals have the knowledge map stored (Reich & Wee, 2006), containing details of what they know about other individual's experiences , as well as subjective insights, intuitions, stories, hunches and other evaluative knowledge. Tacit knowledge transfer is done mostly through joint activities, rather than written or verbal instructions, with social interactions around a problematic situation (Nonaka et al., 1995). Nevertheless, in order to be shared and transferred, it needs to be made explicit so that it is accessible for everyone in the company or the wider spectrum of audience.

In explicit category, the knowledge is presented by researchers in different ways in terms of storage and exchange. This can be considered a *"hard"* way of knowledge transfer, including databases, files, manuals, and written lessons learned. It is more precise and can be articulated. This enables it to be more easily codified, stored, transferred or shared (Nonaka et al., 1995). It represents a more formal and systemic way of knowledge sharing. Accordingly it can be formulized through books, letters, manuals, standard operating procedures and instructions (Polanyi, 1967). Furthermore, it can be categorized into: declarative, procedural and causal knowledge (Zack, 1999 cited by Reich et al., 2006).

When discussing the learning within projects, a special emphasis is given to the project completion phase of the project life cycle, considering that the knowledge of the whole project can be captured and transferred to other projects. The capturing and transferring of knowledge is done through processes. Processes in knowledge management are analyzed in terms of procedures that exist within the project for knowledge transfer and learning (Zollo & Winter, 2001). Moreover, the interactive process of new knowledge development and its integration to existing knowledge within the company, as well as its transfer to the company, it all contributes to enhancing the adaptive capabilities of the company.

More detailed findings in the articles related to the three different categories is presented in the text below, specifically divided for each category. Furthermore, the environment wherein these categories co-exist is presented.

2.2   Project based learning in and between projects

A company learns when it converts: (i) tacit knowledge into explicit knowledge (i.e. externalization), (ii) explicit to explicit (i.e. combination), (iii) explicit to tacit (i.e. internalization) and (iv) tacit to tacit (i.e. Socialization) (Nonaka et al., 1995)(see Figure 2).

FIGURE 2
KNOWLEDGE CREATION AND TRANSFER

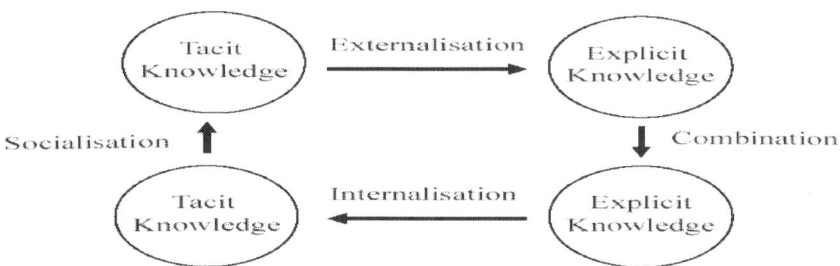

Source: Nonaka & Takeuchi, 1995

As mentioned by Senge (1990, cited by Nonaka et al., 1995, p.45):

"A learning organization is a place where people are continually discovering how they create their reality. And how they can change it"

Project based learning is based more on knowledge integration activities, wherein the concentration is more on specific nature of the task and the composition of the project team. Whilst this generates learning within projects, in terms of definable social group it cannot be applied and transferred to other organizational groups as easily (Prencipe et al., 2001). Nevertheless, project based learning requires a significant investment of resources in terms of money, time, and structures which will be deployed in creating an organizational climate which promotes retaining knowledge.   Also, milestones and deadlines enable inter-functional communication and reflection necessary for wider organizational learning (Lindkvist, Soderlund & Tell, 1998).

Learning through projects is considered a subset of organizational learning, and one of the ways how organizations develop capabilities required to improve their performance. (Davies et al., 2005). Moreover, the sustainable growth and long term profitability in project business depends from the ability to learn from new businesses and convert the knowledge gained into organizational capability to improve project performance. Many

13

companies create learning mechanisms with the attempt to capture the experience gained through projects. However, organizations face challenges in capturing this knowledge (De Fillippi, 2001), because of the loss of the project team members and the inability to transmit the lessons learned effectively and in a timely manner. To avoid loss of this knowledge, there is need for companies to develop and apply a more structured approach which incorporates systematic 'reflective practices' on project experiences (Söderlund, Vaagaasar & Andersen, 2008).

Davies et al., (2005) have concluded based on the empirical studies, that project-based learning should be analyzed and understood as a dynamic process of project capability building. Moreover, they identify a model which consists of two interacting and co-evolving levels of learning, which are:

"Bottom – Up Approach:
- project led-phases of learning;
- Project-to-project phase to capture lessons learned; and
- Project-to-organization phase when the organization increases its capabilities to deliver many projects.

Top-down Approach:
- Business-led learning that occurs when top-down strategic decisions are taken to create and exploit the company-wide resources and capabilities required to perform increasingly predictable and routine project activities. (pp. 185-186)."

Sense (2008) argues that if learning is considered an explicit project action, it can be considered a highly political issue. He elaborates further by taking the example of deliberate learning actions wherein a project team or project manager undertakes a 'public action' (Raelin, 2001, cited in Sense, 2008). According to APM (2006, p.15) the establishment of Project Management Office(s) (PMO) enables the company to *"learn, lead, grow and develop its project management potential by drawing together project management talent."* In addition, the development of human resources from the learning and experience gained by involvement in projects represents a source of *"competitive advantage"* (APM, 2006, p.112).

At the same time, however, it can be argued that the transitory and temporary nature of the projects makes it difficult to embed new organizational learning and knowledge in the well established generic routines and processes within organizations. Attention has been drawn to the examination of the problems faced by project based organizations, in their ability to capture and diffuse cross-project learning (Brady et al., 2003; DeFillippi, 2001; Prencipe et al., 2001). A representation of the reasons why project teams in companies fail to systematically document knowledge and experiences gained on projects are given by Schindler et al.,(2003) (See Table 2).

TABLE 2
REASONS FOR PROJECT TEAM FAILURE TO TRANSFER KNOWLEDGE

> - High time pressure when the project ends (completion pressure and taking over of new tasks)
> - Missing documentation – misplaced ' modesty' (for positive experiences) or fear of negative sanctions (in case of mistakes)
> - Lacking knowledge of debriefing methods
> - Lacking enforcement of the ' debriefing' procedures in project manuals
> - Missing integration of experience recording into project processes
> - Team members do not see a (personal) use of coding experience and assume to address knowledge carriers directly as more efficient
> - Difficulties in coordinating debriefings – persons already engaged in other new projects

Source: Schindler & Eppler (2003)

A number of various strategies can be adopted to overcome the problems outlined Table 2. Support of the senior management and company's no-blame culture is of crucial importance. Moreover, appropriate incentive scheme (intrinsic or extrinsic) needs to be developed to motivate project members to participate in appraisals and knowledge transfer and sharing (Brady et al., 2003). The incentive scheme and the learning mechanisms establishment is the responsibility of qualified project managers, who are considered to be the carriers of the lessons learned in and between projects. Institutionalization of different mechanisms which are accompanied by processes and an appropriate company environment is needed. Knowledge accumulation in a company needs to take into account the tacit and explicit knowledge.

In the following text, the main findings in the articles related to the categories of tacit and explicit knowledge are presented. Also, category of processes is elaborated upon and the company environment the mechanisms of tacit and explicit knowledge and processes co-exist in.

2.3   Tacit Knowledge

Projects are perceived to be seen as knowledge-intensive tasks which can be approached in terms of quantity or quality of knowledge. Today's projects are faced with high levels of complexity and interdependency in and between projects. This creates a need to shift towards an information-based company and a knowledge-creating and sharing environment, thus, motivating people to be actively involved in the knowledge management process (Ayas, 1996).

The need to share tacit knowledge and disseminate best practice represents the need to leverage the knowledge gained by key project team members, therefore making it a company asset, rather that retain the knowledge as individual assets. An information based approach in the development of practice of project management is the solution according to Ayas (1996). She proposes this shift in the project management philosophy, so that a competitive advantage is sustained. In addition, she suggests that the hierarchy structure within projects should be replaced by a team structure, wherein the teams manage themselves, so called the Project Network Structure (PNS). By developing this approach, the possibility arises to improve the processes and mechanisms in and between projects, by building a team to share the experiences.

Capability to learn from the projects conducted in the past is important. Past experience is crucial to sustain success and improvement in projects. Knowledge of the project is the shared knowledge among the team members and project managers, therefore, they need to be integrated effectively and create a knowledge base that is continuously enhanced. This enables people working in projects to transmit their learning to others, considering their constant involvement in the learning process. Baumard (1999) argues that tacit knowledge can be an attribute of individuals, but as well as of groups, collectives or organizations. Mumford (1994) argues that not all companies provide a working environment that encourages learning, and not all managers are willing to learn and change.

Considering that learning is an important factor for project performance, a greater perception and understanding of the significance of each separate phase in the project is needed, and not so much the change of the attitudes of project team members (Mumford,1994). At the same time, the overlaps that happen between the project phases are considered to represent a problem for integration.

The attempt to capture the practitioners experience requires the utilization of company's mechanisms to perform the function of recording, storing and dissemination (Zack, 1999, cited by Reich et al., 2006). Examples of these efforts are: end-of-the project debriefing techniques like Post-Project Appraisals, After Action Reviews, and Post Control. Some of these techniques can be employed at the end of each project phase or stage gate (i.e. Project Audits – Quality Audits, Schedule Audits, and Status Reports) (Gardiner, 2005). Table 3 illustrates the examples of mechanisms for capturing tacit knowledge.

TABLE 3

MECHANISMS FOR CAPTURING TACIT KNOWLEDGE

Mechanism	Author	Year of publishing
Serial, strategic & expert transfer	Dixon	2000
Post-Project Appraisals	Gulliver	1987
After-Action Reviews	Busby	1999
	Roth & Kleiner	1998
Community of practice	Brady et al.,	1998
	Wenger	1998
Team meetings	APM	2006
Knowledge Maps	Reich et al.,	2006
Training	Brady et al.,	1998
Mentoring	APM	2006
	Brady et al.,	1998
Coaching	APM	2006
Forums	Prencipe et al.,	2001
Project histories	Ayas et al.,	2001

Post-Project Appraisals (PPA) (Gulliver, 1987, cited by Schindler et al., 2003), is a way to evaluate and learn from projects after their completion, and gain effective lessons learned. In order to be more objective and credible, the evaluation is done from an external party, after a certain period of time has passed from project completion. The outcome is the dissemination of the lessons learned, detailing the individual and team learning experiences. The external party conducts the interviews, possibly from all the involved team members of the project. Unless this is done in a systematic manner, errors will be repeated, at cost, with no resultant learning.

After Action Reviews (Busby 1999; Roth & Kleiner, 1998, cited by Schindler et al., 2003) is a method that is applied when a complete project evaluation is not possible. It enables the organization to learn immediately from errors and successes. The questions that you try to answer in this case are: What was different and has anything been learned this time? The method to be used is brainstorming and team-learning, building trust and team integrity are crucial to the process.

A community of practice (Brady et al., 2003; Wenger, 1998) provides an environment where people can develop knowledge through interaction with others. Moreover, the environment promotes creation, nurturing and sustainability of knowledge. Accordingly, Williams (2004) encourages creation of communities of practice within a project, so that the knowledge is disseminated, particular attention given to the tacit or complex knowledge. According to APM, the establishment of PMO offices provides *"the infrastructure to support communities of practice"* (APM, 2006, p.15).

Team meetings are also proposed, with an increase in the frequency but a shortening in the duration. Moreover, the key team members share their knowledge on key issues and suggest solutions. Roadblocks, potential issues, risks and risk mitigation strategies are discussed in these meetings (APM, 2006). This is more considered a tacit to tacit creation of knowledge, nevertheless, it can be converted to explicit if the minutes of meetings are taken and distributed accordingly.

Knowledge maps (Reich et al., 2006) are used in tacit knowledge as well as explicit knowledge. In terms of tacit knowledge, it represents a map stored in individuals' minds, containing knowledge of other individuals as well as intuitions, stories, hunches.

Training (Brady et al., 2003) is used to inform and update the project team members that are new, as well as existing staff members on the recent information and changes made to the projects. Formal training is believed to accelerate learning by drawing on the collected experience of those involved in the activity.

Mentoring (APM, 2006; Brady et al., 2003) is considered to be useful way to transfer and enhance experience and knowledge. It is support, guidance and advice provided by one experienced person. It can be formal or informal, but in recent practices it is considered to be more formal, wherein team members consider mentoring an expected activity. Moreover, it can be evaluated at the end of the project in the appraisal forms.

Coaching (APM, 2006) is an initiative to share knowledge. It is a process to address person's development needs and enhance performance while fulfilling the work needed to complete the project. But coaches are sensitive to the preferred learning styles.

Forums (Prencipe et al., 2001) are initiatives wherein the project managers organize monthly or bimonthly events to talk about tools and share the information.

Retreats (Prencipe et al.,2001) are also initiatives undertaken by the management of the companies, wherein different levels of project and program functions are gathered in a location off the company site, in order to discuss the progress and ' lessons learned'. The duration can be 2-3 days, and it can take place approximately once a year.

Dixon (2000) has identified different types of tacit knowledge transfer or reuse: serial transfer, strategic transfer and expert transfer. Serial transfer happens when same group of workers perform the same task and apply their own knowledge to it. Strategic transfer happens when a team is conducting a task that doesn't happen frequently, and want to benefit from other's experience. Expert transfer happens when tacit and explicit knowledge is transferred from the expert source (internal or external to the team), which will help the team solve the problems with the application of new methods and knowledge received. According to Karlsen & Gottschalk (2003) there is a direct correlation between the extent of strategic transfer and project success.

The combination of the stories and experiences, as well as lessons learned expressed in explicit lists and lessons learned reports, deliver the teams memory. Creating and updating a shared memory is an important team activity at the beginning, during and at the end of the project (Schindler et al., 2003). Accordingly, it builds up to the Organizational Memory, which is stored in a system, which serves as a repository of data, information and knowledge, which are retrieved and used to build upon to make new decisions (Hatami & Galliers, cited by Jennex, 2005).

Explicit knowledge is more about how and why things work, whereas tacit knowledge is more about what things work. According to Nonaka et al. (1995), new knowledge is created by an interaction between explicit and tacit knowledge, facilitated through knowledge sharing and socialization. Mooradian (2005) states that explicit knowledge is an extension of tacit knowledge to a new level. Moreover, Nonaka et al. (1995) claim that company's are unaware of the importance of tacit knowledge and the necessity to make it explicit.

Tacit knowledge management and transfer are done with goal of mitigating the risk of loss of knowledge through staff departure. All the resources proposed during the text are options which can be utilized, nevertheless there is no one answer. Each project needs to adapt the resources to be utilized to the specific circumstances it operates in and also to the specific needs of the project and the company in the long term. Except tacit knowledge transfer, an explicit knowledge transfer is conducted, and it complements to the tacit knowledge.

2.4   Explicit knowledge

Explicit knowledge, unlike tacit knowledge, can be embodied in a code or language; therefore, it can be easily communicated and shared. Code incorporates numbers, words, or symbols. Also, Nonaka et al. (1995) claim that explicit knowledge can be expressed in words and numbers, and easily communicated and shared in the form of hard data, scientific formulae, codified procedures or universal principles. The fact that explicit knowledge is documented, public, structured, and of fixed content, makes it easier to be captured and shared through IT.

Cooper et al., (2002) states that the problem of not learning from previous projects or between projects lies in identifying what had a positive impact, how to codify and share, and how to improve after these lessons given. Many companies consider it a good practice to create a documented account on what has been learned in a project. Systematic approach to project learning can be a competence for a company and therefore give a sustainable competitive advantage (Schindler et al., 2003). Examples are manuals and computer-based tools. However, even though this practice is routine, it is difficult to find that the resulting document has been actually referenced in the next project.

Liikamma (2006) states that although most methodologies recommend that work packages exist for securing knowledge and experiences, they are often not included in the overall project plan. Therefore, effective knowledge management needs to be included and mentioned explicitly in the project plan, in order to be considered significant by project team members (APM, 2008). Accordingly, time and resources need to be assigned specifically to the task dealing with project knowledge management.

TABLE 4
MECHANISMS FOR CAPTURING EXPLICIT KNOWLEDGE

Mechanism	Author	Year of publishing
Lessons learned systems	Owen & Burstein, in Jennex	2005
Micro Articles	Wilke,in Schindler et al.,	2003
Learning History	Roth et al.,	1998
Project Reviews	APM	2006
Knowledge Maps	Davenport et al.,	1998
Knowledge Inventory	Reich et al.,	2006
Simulations	APM	2006
	Lambe	2004
Electronic based news	Coakes, Bradburn & Blake, in Jennex	2005
Project transfer matrix	Hahn, Schmiedinger & Stephan, in Jennex	2005
Knowledge based risk assessment systems	APM	2004
Project histories	Ayas et al.,	2001

Resources necessary for lessons learned systems and codification include collection, archiving, analyzing, processing, dissemination and research. Then in order to be transferred throughout the project based company, the lessons learned products are published, such as bulletins, newsletters, handbooks, and Internet (APM, 2008). Without access to lessons learned, the project team will lack important knowledge of the project's risks and the opportunity to share information as to how these risks can impact the project targets. At the same time, the team members using the systems need to be aware of its benefits and need to be encouraged to use them.

Lessons learned systems (Owen & Burstein, cited in Jennex, 2005) encapsulate the lessons learned (both formal and informal) during the project, which are done by the team members of the project or sometimes through independent reviewers. They provide a full description of the project, detailing the specific useful examples to be applied in future projects. Nevertheless, there is a need to focus not only on the success parts of the project (Disteter, 2002) but also on the failure (negative parts). And for an easy access and to be retrievable for the future, they are put and updated in the specific systems. This is considered a tacit to explicit knowledge creation and transfer, which is available on the network server (i.e. database). In addition, Kotnour (2000) claims that for the successfulness of the project, the "lessons learned" should be produced during the project and not only at the end of the project.

Micro Articles (Wilke, 1998, cited by Schindler et al., 2003) are used to capture and secure experience after project completion, therefore, making knowledge explicit. It is an informal written style, to a length of maximum one page.

Learning History (Roth et al., 1998, cited by Schindler et al., 2003) is a written storytelling approach, describing the main events from the project, presented in chronological order. Its length ranges from twenty to hundred pages, based on the length and complexity of the project. It represents the tacit knowledge of the team members, considering that it is directly written by the team members, incorporating their statements and mistakes.

Project reviews (APM, 2006, pp.90-91) are independent checks on a project's progress, which *"ensures that a particular project is on track and it can proceed with full management support."*. A phase review within the project can be conducted, to ensure that the project is relevant to the company, and *"it adheres to policies and procedures"* (APM, 2008, p.16). It is based on the key project milestones, and it identifies and manages risk. Also, it enables the project manager and project team to reflect on the project and objectively review their work. In addition, upon completion of the project a review can be conducted to ensure that the benefits are being realized by the project and organization. In the post-project review, *"the project is evaluated against its success criteria",* individual and team performance is recognized and project management processes as well as tools and techniques are evaluated (APM, 2006, p.91).

Knowledge maps (Davenport et al., 1998, cited in Woo, Clayton, Johnson, Flores & Ellis. 2004; Grant, 2006, cited by Reich, 2007) are used not only in tacit but also in explicit knowledge for localizing explicit knowledge i.e. documents and databases. It can be possessed by an individual or a group. It differs from knowledge inventory because in addition to containing knowledge about the team, it includes less specific knowledge such as person's ability to lead a team and working environment. Knowledge map allows the individual to ask for guidance in a timely manner to include all relevant considerations and therefore to improve solutions (Reich et al., 2006).

Knowledge inventory (Reich et al., 2006), is a sort of database, which contains the information on the skills and knowledge's of each team member, such as their education, projects completed, and industry experience. Accordingly, it is the knowledge that already exists within the teams and is available to the team as well as the gaps and deficiencies. It can be accessed and utilized by the authorized project team members. It can take the form of Human Yellow Pages.

Simulations (APM, 2008; Lambe, 2004) are better tool considering that a wide number of variables can be incorporated. Moreover, it enables the team members to experience the consequences of their actions through time, by simulating events through time. This creates an environment wherein the team members can be prepared for changing circumstances, as well as learn in advance what the expected events will be based on the actions they undertake.

Electronic based news (Coakes, Bradburn & Blake, cited by Jennex, 2005) is also a tool to be utilized, which is an electronic, interactive publication summarizing the latest innovations, legislation and practice on the respective field required and it is usually available on the shared internet portal of the company. It can also provide links to external websites for industry best-practices via Internet. The companies can also send it to their staff once in two weeks, or once a month, depending on the necessity to be updated.

Project Transfer Matrix (Hahn, Schmiedinger & Stephan, cited by Jennex, 2005) is a knowledge management tool used for efficient planning, controlling and managing the transfer of project results. Table 5 illustrates all the necessary columns containing the necessary information for the transfer.

TABLE 5
PROJECT TRANSFER MATRIX

Project Steps	Executing Division	Output	Status in %	Transfer Relevance	Transfer Complexity	Transfer Responsibility

Source: Hahn et al., cited by Jennex, 2005

Knowledge based risk assessment systems' (APM, 2004, pp. 104) consists of risk assessment models which utilize the knowledge base created from previous models. The key advantage in using these systems is that assessments are made during the early phase of the project, aiding the risk identification.

People need to get used to the idea of knowledge sharing and collective learning. Processes and modern technology needs to be put into place. This is also supported by Hameri et al. (1998) who emphasize the need for clear definitions and well-documented processes to be adopted by project based companies. There needs to be more reliance on data and strict documentation rules, and less on informal networks and informal knowledge. Therefore, a culture that encourages the use of knowledge management systems to complement tacit knowledge and informal networks needs to be implemented. Schindler et al. (2003) also concluded the need for project organizations to adopt formalized structures within their projects to promote learning.

The use of databases is encouraged, wherein project knowledge is stored, and indexed in order to be easily retrieved and used. The technological applications developed for knowledge management aim at substituting human activity and knowledge with rule-based systems that can aid, or perform, problem solving (Davenport et al., 1998). Training needs to be provided on how to utilize the databases, for the smooth running and utilization of the database. Accordingly, Hameri & Nihtilä (1998) have concluded that the use of the database learning has a positive effect on learning, by providing the organization with a deeper understanding of the actual development process through visualization of the data collected.

In projects, the problem of learning can be solved with two propositions. At first, learning and knowledge management needs to be introduced as a part of the project plan, wherein specific resources and time is allocated to them. Then, in order to have a successful development process, utilization of a modern IT system is necessary. The organizational transfer from learning happens by assigning key individuals to projects and by formalizing and institutionalizing the lessons learned from successful projects (Brown & Eisenhardt, 1996 cited by Hameri et al.,, 1998; Nonaka et al., 1995).

Nevertheless, when knowledge sharing is conducted within projects and generally in organizations, particular attention needs to be paid to the methods and modes used (Li, Yezhuang, & Pong, cited by Jennex, 2005). If there are different methods adopted for transferring the same knowledge, this can impact the effectiveness. Therefore, more attention needs to be paid to selection of the right modes for organizational learning and training in explicit knowledge sharing. Benefits gained from accumulated tacit and explicit knowledge are: enhanced project competences, reduced costs due to avoiding repetition of mistakes, reduced project risks, better coordination and enhanced competitiveness (Cooper et al., 2002; Kotnour, 1999). The tacit and explicit knowledge transfer is done through processes. A detailed understanding of what are the collective processes used for developing knowledge that can be reused in other activities and projects is needed. Processes are elaborated in the following text.

2.5 Processes

According to Müller (2009, p.3) *"governance needs to be put in place in an organization to provide a framework for managerial action"* by setting the boundaries for management action and defining the processes that managers should use to run their areas of responsibility.

APM Body of Knowledge (2006) advocates four categories of project management processes that need to be applied to each phase of the project life cycle. They are:
- A starting or initiating process;
- A defining and planning process;
- A monitoring and controlling process; and
- A learning and closing process (APM, 2006, p.3).

Processes in the knowledge management are analyzed in the context of procedures in which the projects are conducted concerning learning and knowledge transfer. The underpinning theoretical perspective is that project competencies are built-up through various learning processes. The learning process in the companies can be in the dimensions of 'single loop' learning and 'double loop' learning (Harvey, Palmer, & Speier, 1998). Except for "single loop" learning – where members in organization identify the mismatch between intentions and outcomes – the need for 'double loop' learning also emerges in organizations. This enables the organizations to question and confront the routines and create new; more appropriate ones thereby resonating strongly with organizational change (Argyris, 1999). Recognition of need to encourage continuous learning – single and double loop- within the corporate strategy has also been identified important in the studies of Hameri et al., (1998) and Schindler et al., (2003).

The project management processes integrate all the necessary parts. With the definition of inputs and outputs, while considering the constraints and mechanisms, it provides a single point of integration of all relevant parts. This is illustrated with Figure 3.

FIGURE 3
THE PROJECT MANAGEMENT PROCESS

Constraints
Time, cost, quality, technical and other performance parameters, legal, environment, etc

Input
Business need, problem or opportunity

Management of the project

Output
Project deliverables and/ or services, change

Mechanisms
People, tools and techniques and equipment, organization

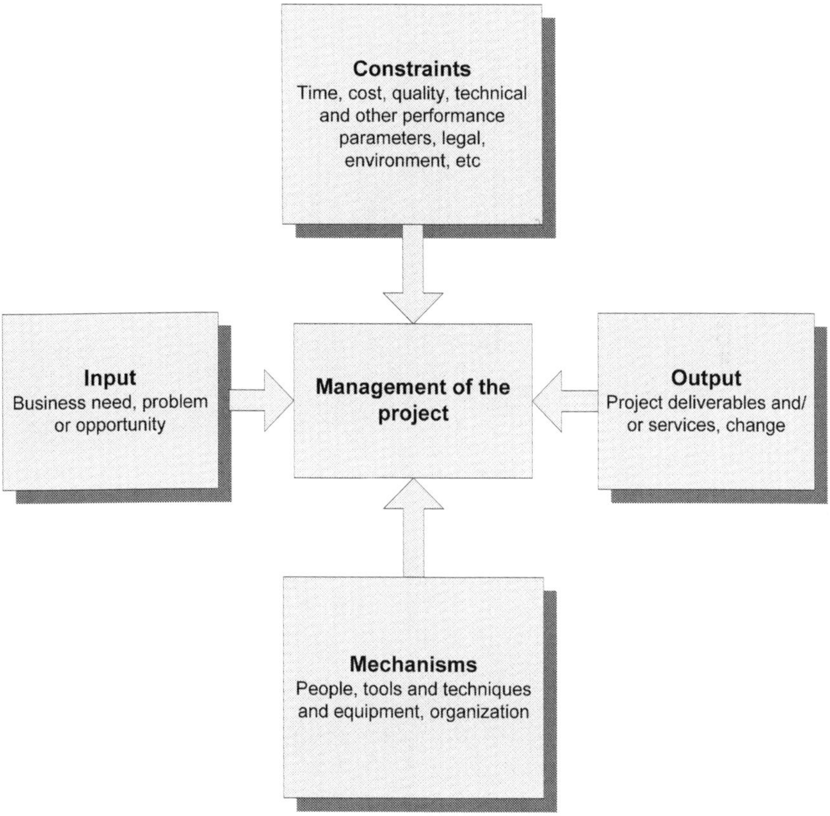

Source: (APM BOK, 2006, p. 3)

The interactive process of developing new knowledge and integrating it with existing organizational knowledge, and transferring it to the whole company enhances the adaptive capabilities of the company. It is consisted of continuous process in reconfiguration, re-combinations and continuous upgrading of operating routines and company resources, which leads to new product/service offerings that keep-up with changes in the market place. A process flow diagram is provided by PMBOK (2004) representing a summary of process inputs and outputs that flow down through all the processes within a specific knowledge (See Figure 4).

FIGURE 4
PROCESS FLOW DIAGRAM LEGEND

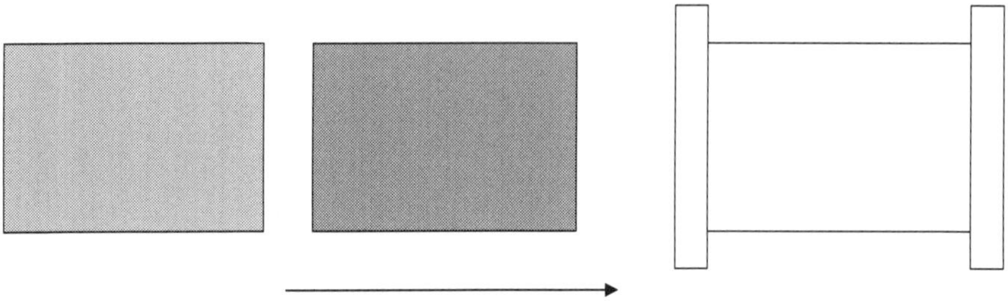

Process within   Process outside of   External to Process
knowledge area   knowledge area

Process Flow diagram shows basic steps and interactions.

Source: (PMBOK, 2004, p. 73)

One of the knowledge management processes that can be used in projects in terms of tacit knowledge is personalization (Koskinen, 2004; Koskinen, Pihlanto & Vanharanta, 2003). In personalization, the center is the individual. Knowledge is tied to one person in this case, and its only possibility to share is only through person-to-person contacts. For example, the skills of a top manager cannot be learned from a textbook or in class, but only through years of experience.

The knowledge management process used in explicit knowledge is codification (Koskinen et al., 2003). With codification, the center is the computers. The knowledge is codified, and transferred into the databases, which can be accessed and used by authorized team members of the project. At the same time, considering that it is represented in writing the flow of the knowledge goes from the project management to the individual team members. Accordingly, the knowledge can be sent to people involved in vast distances. Moreover, when knowledge is codified, the transfer will increase and costs associated with such transfer will decrease (Cowan & Foray, 1997). On the other hand, even the codified knowledge can be subject to alternative interpretations, which creates difficulty in knowing when to use this knowledge in a problem-solving situation (Koskinen, 2004). Although the impact of codification for the efficiency of organizational processes needs further study, researchers mostly concentrate on the importance of outcomes of codification leaving the cognitive process accompanied with it unexplored. Zollo et al., (2001) emphasize the relevance and importance of the process dimension of knowledge codification.

Learning process is facilitated with the usage of project reviews, wherein the knowledge acquired from project execution is captured in project phase reports and closeout reports. This accumulated knowledge is then deposited into the company knowledge base (i.e. different databases the companies employ) (Brady et al., 2004). Moreover, it is important not to forget the tacit knowledge which is not captured in the written reports. Therefore, the usage of story telling, project history etc. is used for facilitating tacit knowledge transfer. This knowledge transfer needs to be conducted in a no-blame environment, wherein appropriate solutions can be proposed and implemented.

The 'lessons learned' from and during the planning and execution of projects in the past can be referenced for project planning and execution of a project in the future. Therefore, project competences of a project in the future are enhanced from the successes and failures experienced in past projects. Furthermore, the new project after completion will produce 'lessons learned' which will contribute to other future projects. The process of learning in projects shows us that project has two roles: (i) utilize past projects knowledge to improve current and future projects, and (ii) upgrade the accumulated 'knowledge base' with new lessons learned from ongoing projects (Lampel, Scarbrough & Macmillan, 2008).

Based on Zollo and Winter (2001), the model of learning consists of three processes that occur in the company: (i) experience accumulation, (ii) knowledge articulation, and (iii) knowledge codification. Then the mechanisms which are utilized by companies in each of the processes are identified. The companies choose the specific process depending on the task they want to learn. Their research concludes that the lower the frequency (temporary nature) and the higher the heterogeneity (uniqueness) of the task, the more effective knowledge articulation and codification is. A Three-by-Three matrix is designed by Prencipe et al., (2001) to discover a learning landscape that a company uses. Based on the processes that the companies use more, a learning landscape is created. This will be utilized in the analysis of the data.

Learning typologies are different for each knowledge process used. In experience accumulation the concentration is on expertise of individuals. In knowledge articulation the performance is considered and it involves two-way communication. And, knowledge codification is mostly focused on applying the knowledge in paper so that it can be stored and re-used. A more detailed elaboration on the learning typologies, outcomes and economic benefits related to the three processes are presented in Table 6.

TABLE 6
LEARNING TYPOLOGIES, OUTCOMES AND ECONOMIC BENEFITS

	Learning Processes		
	Experience accumulation	Knowledge articulation	Knowledge codification
Learning typologies	• Learning by doing • Learning by using	• Learning by reflecting • Learning by thinking • Learning by discussing • Learning by confronting	• Learning by writing and re-writing • Learning by implementing • Learning by replicating • Learning by adapting
Outcomes	• Local experts and experiential knowledge in individuals (e.g. subject matter expert)	• Improved understanding of action-performance relation (predictive knowledge) • Symbolic representation and communication	• Codified manuals, procedures (e.g. project management process)
Economic benefits	• Economics of specialization	• Economics of co-ordination	• Economics of information (diffusion, replication, and reuse of information)

Source: Prencipe & Tell, 2001, p. 29

The sole focus on the information storing and capturing of information and communication technologies (ICTs) leads to a static view of knowledge in organizations, but the way it has come to the information and how it is used seems to be forgotten. Therefore, an understanding of which are the processes in project based companies involved in the management of knowledge is needed. Moreover, the environment that the processes and mechanisms for knowledge transfer co-exists in needs to be analyzed, considering that it provides an arena for these mechanisms and processes to be institutionalized.

2.6   Company Environment

Sense (2007) argues on the need to understand and appreciate the complexity of the learning process and how it is impacted by the project environment (within and outside the project). Moreover, he argues for developing the appropriate *'social infrastructures' which are 'practical, locally relevant and participant-oriented'* (p.411). According to Kotnour (2000), the organization needs to create an environment which empowers team members, who are allowed to admit mistakes and openly discus solutions to the presented problem. APM (2006) supports this by encouraging the organization to foster a culture of improvement and frank disclosure of project information. Carillo, Robinson, Al-Ghassani & Anumba (2004), claim that an inappropriate company environment, the hierarchy structure, represents barriers to effective project knowledge management.

The popular view among project managers is that "*we don't do culture, a strategy and a plan is everything*". But in Ford company it is explicitly stated that "culture eats strategy for breakfast" (Pritchard, cited by APM, 2008, p.19). According to Pritchard, it is important to create a culture and environment where asking difficult and challenging questions is appreciated and encouraged. Moreover, an appreciation needs to be developed on the emotional ground including the company histories, and the effects of previous events.

An environment analysis needs to be done in the context of where project management takes place. The structure of the company defines "*the reporting and decision-making hierarchy of an organization*" and how project management operates within it (APM, 2006, p. 92). If the environment in which the project management takes place is wrongly assessed, the project team might be either over or under challenged. Accordingly, they might apply the processes and procedures which are inappropriate to the current situation, or might consider that the use of processes for knowledge management is useless.

Bayer, Enparantza, Maier, Obermair & Schmiedinger (cited by Jennex, 2005) goes beyond by proposing a decentralized knowledge management system, which will promote utilization of tacit knowledge as well as ease the process of converting tacit knowledge into explicit knowledge. Moreover, its usage enables the individual knowledge people to actively participate in and share the benefits of knowledge management system. Therefore, the integration of e-mails, instant messaging needs to be done within the knowledge management system, which is not done in a centralized knowledge management system. And, it reduces the costs of implementation and maintenance of the knowledge management system.

Sense (2008) has explored the conditioning of project participants to learn within a project environment. The term 'conditioning' refers to how elements of socio-cultural environment of the project impact the participants' authority to want to or to be able to pursue learning activity. He concluded that in an environment where "higher authority" is present, people defer to it for guidance and decision-making rather than operating in a more self-driven and independent fashion.

Schein (1992) has proposed a cultural perspective to analysis of environment that creates an arena for knowledge transfer and learning. He emphasized the fact that cultural changes within a company need to be supported by primary culture-embedding mechanisms and also articulation and reinforcement mechanisms. An attempt to relate the initiatives of a company with the culture-embedding and articulation/reinforcement mechanisms is presented in Table 7.

TABLE 7
CULTURE EMBEDDING AND ARTICULATION/REINFORCMENT MECHANISMS

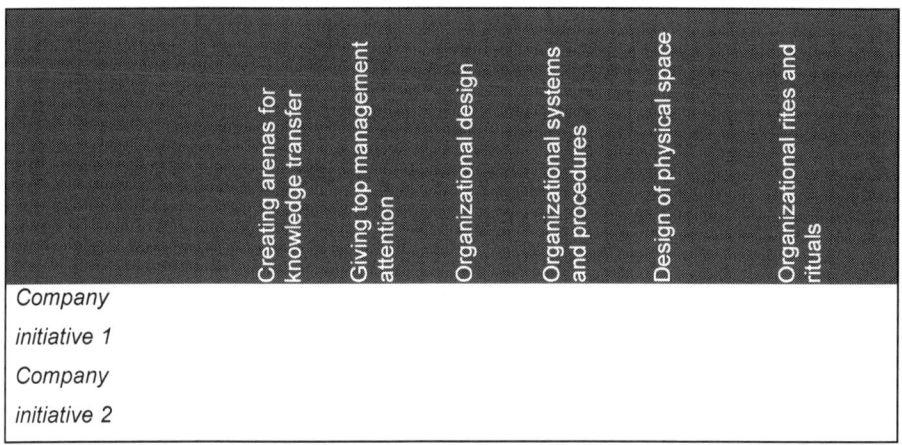

	Creating arenas for knowledge transfer	Giving top management attention	Organizational design	Organizational systems and procedures	Design of physical space	Organizational rites and rituals
Company initiative 1						
Company initiative 2						

Source: Schein, 1992, p.116

According to Brady at al., (2003) the benefits of a no-blame culture enable the companies to direct their energy at correcting the mistakes and attempting to prevent something similar happening in the future rather than apportioning blame. Another important side of the environment is not only from the management side. It is important to consider how people receive a knowledge sharing environment. Some people are reluctant to share their knowledge and some are unwilling to act on information that was provided by someone else, which is the 'not-invented here' syndrome (Brady et al., 2003). The ethos for sharing knowledge needs to be deeply embedded within the people working in the organization, because it benefits the organization as a whole.

2.7   Summary of categories

The three categories see the importance of having an environment that promotes knowledge transfer and encourages learning. A need for knowledge management shift is recognized, wherein managers realize the importance of knowledge transfer and learning in project performance. The categories emphasize different mechanisms and processes on how to increase knowledge transfer and improve learning.

Some researchers emphasize the importance of having more mechanisms and processes, whereas other emphasizes the change in the company environment. This is more applicable to explicit knowledge category, which can be codified and processes can be applied. Nevertheless, the tacit knowledge category is more theoretical and is harder to be put in practice and implemented by practitioners (Nonaka et al., 1995). Articles do not have a similar saying on what the most important factors for knowledge transfer and learning are. Different articles propose a different combination of mechanisms and processes. Also the environment wherein these mechanisms and processes co-exist is considered as crucial in some of the articles.

Although many companies attempt to efficiently and effectively manage and transfer the knowledge throughout the project-based company, there have been few attempts at identifying how different companies themselves manage and transfer the knowledge. This study aims at contributing to the fulfillment of this gap, by addressing the processes and mechanisms as well as experiences of project professionals in managing and transferring knowledge in Case Company X, a company located in UK. Also the environment and conditions which promotes learning in projects will be elaborated upon.

2.8   Research Propositions

The reviewed articles were not able to answer the research question stated in the study. The categorization of the tacit, explicit knowledge and processes has been proven important to learning and knowledge transfer in and between projects. Also the environment these categories co-exist in has been proven significant in the project success and increased performance in projects. From the literature reviewed the researcher has identified that knowledge transfer and learning consists of tacit knowledge and explicit knowledge. Moreover, the conversion of tacit knowledge into explicit is done with application of appropriate processes. Additionally, the environment where the projects are conducted plays a crucial role. This study will look at to what extend and in what form are these categories and project-based learning present in Case Company X.

The results of the empirical study will provide an approach to answering the research question.

By the end of the study, the following results are expected:

a) The study will show that there is a difference between the current practices for knowledge transfer and learning in Case Company X and the practices suggested by literature.
b) There will be a number of suggestions proposed on how to increase knowledge transfer and improve learning in and between projects within Company X in UK.

3. METHODOLOGY

The research is composed of three sources of data:

i)   Literature review which gives the theoretical background related to the knowledge transfer and learning; the focus is on the mechanisms used for tacit and explicit knowledge, the processes and the environment they co-exist in.

ii) A search and review of Case Company X specific secondary data sources, such as governance sets within Case Company X, policy documents, company's best practices in relation to knowledge sharing and transfer.

iii) Semi-structured interviews with different levels of project personnel within the division of programme management in Case Company X.

The usage of multiple sources is done with the goal of eliminating bias and minimizing errors of the data findings, by applying triangulation (Bryman and Bell, 2003). In this chapter research philosophy, approach, layout, data collection, data reduction, display, conclusion, reliability and validity applied to achieve the research objective are elaborated at a greater detail.

3.1 Research Philosophy

The research philosophy is the guide to developing knowledge during the research (Saunders, Lewis & Thornhill, 2003). The determination of research methodology is interlinked with ontology and epistemology. Ontology is the science of study of being in existence, whereas epistemology is the study of knowledge, science, model and testability (Bryman et al., 2003).

Within ontology, there are two main sciences: positivism and interpretivism (Bryman et al., 2003; Saunders et al., 2003). The positivist approach holds that the goal of knowledge is to describe the phenomenon that is experienced (Trochim, 2006). A positivist believes that the world is external and objective. The world can be measured through objective methods (i.e. facts and observations). The end- product of positivism can be law-like generalization similar to those produced by the physical and natural scientist (Remenyi, Williams, Money, and Swartz, 1998). The theory in positivism is developed with establishing a hypothesis and deducing the information which supports or rejects the hypothesis.

The interpretivism approach acknowledges that complexity of the insights in a field cannot be generalized, especially in business and management research, wherein the situations are unique and specific to the individual and the circumstances they co-exist in (Saunders et al., 2003). The interpretist approach understands the experience of people, through investigating how they use language and symbols. Researcher's emphasis is on "making sense" on what is happening, which enables generation of findings beyond existing scientific explanations and knowledge (Bryman et al., 2003; Blumberg, Cooper & Schindler, 2005). Human interaction in the environment cannot be ignored, and it has considerable impact on the data collection process of a research.

Given the nature of the research question, the study will be conducted from an interpretivism perspective utilizing qualitative analysis techniques. Interpretivism will enable the researcher to discover the details of the situation to understand the reality (Remenyi et al., 1998). The goal of the undertaken study is to achieve a greater understanding of how the understanding and perception of learning and knowledge transfer can contribute and impact the implementation and performance of the project(s).

This directs the reader to epistemology, which is the science of knowledge and knowing, pertaining to philosophy (Bryman et al., 2003). It is concerned with analyzing knowledge and its relation to truth and belief. It raised the questions as to how knowledge is created, how do people know what they know, etc. Within epistemology, there are also different ends. On one end there is the older epistemological view on knowledge, being the positivistic understanding of truth, which is an objective view and considered absolute. On the other end, there is a different understanding view of knowledge – hermeneutic view- which considers the specifics of the situation. Immediately a similarity can be noticed between the positivism ontology and objective epistemology, as well as interpretivism ontology and hermeneutic epistemology (Ginev, 1995). Therefore, a hermeneutic approach to knowledge is adopted, which enables one to illustrate individual perceptions and interpretations of reality. The study has a hermeneutic view because the purpose is to understand how learning and knowledge transfer is used in project management.

A qualitative approach is adapted in this case study, because the researcher wants to see and grasp the reality from the interviewees' point of view. The qualitative method is a process where the researcher and the respondent interact (Bryman et al., 2003). Therefore, the research is perceived as a communication process and the interviewees (i.e. the researcher's object) are perceived as the subject(s). The project management mechanisms, processes and environment are seen from the project managers and programme managers' perspective, which contributes to the increase of understanding of their purpose and complexity.

3.2   Research Approach

According to Byrne (2001) methodology links the philosophy to the appropriate research process, tools and techniques serving as a bridge between the philosophical notions and the practical research strategies.

There are two main research approaches for empirical reality: deductive and inductive. In the deductive approach, conclusions are drawn based on logical information. It works from more general to more specific reasoning, through weak hypothesis and their testing. After creating the theoretical base, empirical data is collected.   And the theoretical framework is already in place as a starting point, which is used to compare the findings with the theory (Glaser & Strauss, 1967). In the inductive approach, conclusions are drawn from the empirical data to change, complement or confirm existing theories. In this case the reasoning is opposite of deductive, going from more specific to more general. Therefore, first the empirical observations are conducted. Patterns are identified during the analysis of the data process, and the ending is in the form of theory and propositions(Bryman et al., 2003).

This case study is based on an inductive approach wherein the theory/idea is generated from the data collected at Case Company X –UK. Case study approach allows for exploration and interpretation of meanings and contributes to changing in practice (Bryman et al., 2003). The researcher in this study wants to interpret the people's words during the interviews. Therefore, a hermeneutic approach, qualitative data and inductive approach will be applied in this case study. The inductive approach enables the researcher to interpret a situation in its context, through discovering a more comprehensive framework for mechanisms and processes used for knowledge transfer and learning. Moreover, it will be understood how knowledge transfer and learning is carried out at Case Company X in UK compared to what theory proposes.

The data from primary and/or secondary resources are of a subjective nature, presented from the perspective of the source (i.e. interviewee) and the understanding of the researcher conducting the study. After the development of a broad theoretical knowledge base on knowledge mechanisms and learning, the researcher proceeds to search of governance documents and best practices specific to knowledge management under Case Company X jurisdiction. The secondary data are complemented with the primary data extracted from the interviews with the project and programme managers. The researcher seeks to 'triangulate' the data and draw un-bias conclusions, and therefore minimize the error factor. The practices for knowledge transfer and learning in Case Company X are confirmed with a higher degree of credibility, considering that data is coming from three sources.

3.3   Research Strategy

Bryman et al., (2003) discuss two clusters of research strategy: quantitative and qualitative. Quantitative research is based on quantification of data, while the qualitative research is based on words. The major differences are presented in Table 8 . The researcher applied the qualitative research strategy.

TABLE 8
QUANTITATIVE VS. QUALITATIVE RESEARCH STRATEGY

	Quantitative	Qualitative
Research Philosophy	Positivism	Interpretivism
Research Approach	Deductive Testing Theory	Inductive Generating Theory
Nature of social entities	Objectivism (Social reality is independent of social actors)	Constructionism (Social reality is developed through interaction and is constantly emerging)

Source: Bryman and Bell, 2003

3.4   Data Collection

The essence of empirical evidence is to produce and accumulate evidence to support the findings of the research. Moreover, several approaches can be used to collect evidence, and which choice you make is dependable on the research question (Remenyi et al., 1998).

Data collection was done through seven interviews. This provided qualitative data on the categories the research was exploring. An elaboration of Access to data, Interviews, Interview guide and critique of the sources is given.

3.4.1 Access to data

The approached company initiated the idea of an MSc student conducting a research topic as part of their knowledge sharing initiative, therefore they were willing to provide all the necessary information to achieve the best outcome. It seems the respondents that were approached had a positive attitude and gave their maximal contribution. The topic chosen seemed to be viewed important and their desire is to improve the knowledge and learning within their company. It seems that before the topic was chosen by the company, it was noticeable that a considerable amount of thought has been given, and time has been invested. The researcher was presented with a list of seven interviewees who were willing to respond to questions. Therefore, all the seven interviews were conducted during the four weeks stay of the researcher in the Case Company X premises in UK. It was not considered necessary to conduct more than seven interviews, because the results were coherent. In addition, Case Company X has given access to the templates and the governance set documentation, concentrating mainly on knowledge transfer and learning mechanisms and processes.

Case Company X has achieved a leading role in the market, and is nowadays in the top ten list of the major UK companies. To achieve this position, they thought it is a requirement to apply a set of routines, mechanisms and processes for their programme/project division. Therefore, the researcher found it reasonable to talk to people involved only in the programme division within Case Company X, considering their experience in project management. Contacts were made with different levels of project/programme titles, ranging from Project Manager to Senior Programme Manager. The respondents were previously informed on the visit of the MSc student, which visit actually was considered as a small scale project within the non-delivery projects of Programme Development & Finance Office (PDFO). All the respondents reacted positively to the topic and the idea, and were very keen to contribute with the hope that the outcome might give valuable recommendations. Considering that the researcher's visit was organized by PDFO, they prepared the list of interviewees and provided the recording device. The list of the interviewees was decided based on their experience for getting a greater understanding of the project work in the company, and knowledge transfer and learning. Moreover, the interviews were concentrated on people with managerial responsibilities who had an experience and understanding of project management. Their educational background was mostly in engineering, but within Case Company X they were working within different types of programmes/projects. All the persons who were contacted responded positively to the interview invitations, and there were no difficulties of any kind that surfaced.

The researcher contacted the respondents with an introductory email in order to inform them about the context and importance of the research purpose. In the email, the research question and the research objectives were explained, and they were asked to set a time for the interview subject to their availability. The researcher wanted to tape the interviews and there were no objections expressed from the respondents' side. The recording of the interview was done with the purpose of concentrating on what the respondent was saying, rather than on taking notes. The researcher was present at the interviews, and in the beginning of the interview the respondents were given more detailed information on the purpose of the interview, the major sections or content and how it will be used in the future.

3.4.2 The interviews

The primary empirical part of the research was the interviews. It is a common method used for collecting data in the interpretivism approach (Bryman et al., 2003). There are three types of interviews which the researcher can choose: structured, semi-structured and unstructured (Remenyi et al., 1998). In structured interviews a set of questions are pre-determined and identical. In semi-structured interviews, a set of questions is prepared beforehand, but during the conversation new questions can arise. In unstructured interviews, the interview takes form of an informal conversation.

In this case study, semi-structured interviews were applied, wherein the researcher was flexible to change the order of the questions depending on the flow of the interview. The researcher relied on interviewees' perception (Lawrence & Lorsch, 1967). The interviewer was able to explore her area of interest, as well as the interviewee was able to emphasize his/her particular area which they found particularly important or relevant. The aim of the interviews was to engage the management in an investigation process concerning the topic of knowledge transfer and learning. The effects of knowledge transfer of the initiatives investigated were not quantified. Instead there were qualitative assessments of the initiatives during the research period.

A total of 7 interviews took place over a period of four weeks. The semi-structured interviews were held at the Case Company X premises. They took the form of the informal discussion where the researcher provided the key topics she wanted to research in her study. The topics were concentrated on the mechanisms for transmitting tacit and explicit knowledge, the processes and the environment they co-exist in. The interviews lasted for one hour. The interview guide (see Appendix B) was designed based on the theoretical knowledge in literature review and company publications such as governance set and policies. The researcher used open questions because they enable a deeper discussion with the respondent. The questions were posed in a logical order, in order to cover all the necessary topics during the one hour. The logic behind questions enabled follow-up questions. Table 9 represents the list of the interviews successfully conducted. The respondents preferred anonymity; therefore, the description of positions was given rather than names. This layer interview design was explicitly planned to gather data on the same topics from different hierarchical levels in the company, with the possibility of divergent perceptions. Also, they were chosen in order to analyze and identify the typology of knowledge transfer and learning mechanisms that characterized each level. In addition, the processes were identified which accompany the knowledge transfer mechanisms. Relevant company documentation was also consulted. The name of the programmes was not disclosed for security reasons.

TABLE 9
LIST OF INTERVIEWEES

Respondent #	Programme within Case Company X	Title of Respondent
1	Programme 1	PMO Manager
2	Programme 5	Project Manager
3	Programme 2	Senior Programme Manager
4	Programme 3	Quality Manager
5	Programme 4	Executive Director
6	Programme 5	Programme Specialist
7	Programme 6	Senior Programme Manager

The quantity of responses was considered satisfactory by the researcher, considering the theoretical saturation, wherein additional interviews conducted would not add up to more relevant knowledge. Upon obtaining the respondent's feedback which the researcher felt was in line with the scope and requirements of her research aim, the interview were ended and were followed by the collection and analysis of data. Sampling approach used was theoretical sampling. It is an emergent sampling, the same as the theory developed being emergent (Glaser & Strauss, 1967). The emerging theory was defined by the properties of the categories, and their relationship.

3.4.3 The interview guide

The researcher used a one page interview guide (Appendix B) to make sure that all the categories described in the literature review were covered. While conducting the interviews, clarifications were made on unclear questions and sometimes follow-up questions arose. The guide represented a frame for the interviews. During the interview, an attempt was made to steer the discussion in the direction of the established categories. The interview commenced most often with the personal background of the respondent, providing their experience within Case Company X. Thereafter, the other topics were discussed accordingly. Data from these interviews were elaborated to produce the study of Case Company X enabling the identification, evaluation and matching of patterns as they emerged from within individual interviews. The researcher analyzed the recorded interview afterwards and if there were any further clarifications needed, the interviewees were contacted by phone or e-mail. Furthermore, the copy of a finalized dissertation was made available for those involved in the process, as well as a business format report for internal usage of Case Company X.

3.4.4 Literature review and secondary data research

The researcher conducted the search for academic and practitioner literature review to develop a framework for the research. The literature review was done to build internal validity and raise the theoretical level. The collected data was analyzed in the light of the questions raised based on the literature review. Moreover, other research topic specific governance documents as well as best practice guidance of Case Company X were utilized. The list of the governance and policy documents from Case Company X cannot be disclosed due to the non-disclosure agreement signed.

3.4.5 Critique of primary and secondary sources

The researcher is aware of the information which could have been not shared by the respondent during the interviews. The reasons behind this could have been that they are commercially sensitive information not made to be shared. Moreover, the usage of a dictaphone to record the interviews could have intimidated the respondents.

Secondary sources also have limitations, considering the fact that certain criteria were imposed on secondary sources which might have caused one to overlook other sources that could have contributed to the research. Moreover, some of the documents and access to database of Case Company X were not available considering propriety, confidentiality and security of the sensitive information.

3.5 Data Reduction

The researcher had to reduce the data received during the interviews. According to Miles & Huberman (1994), data reduction refers to the process of selecting, focusing, simplifying, abstracting and transforming the data collected. The researcher reduced the data by analyzing the taped interviews and the secondary documentation provided to her by Case Company X. For the interviews the focus was to write down the respondent's statements on the categories of mechanisms of tacit and explicit knowledge, processes as well as the company environment they co-exist in. This enabled the representation of data in the Data Display. The interview, after it was put on paper by the researcher, was sent to the respondents for further comments and approval before being incorporated in the final dissertation. This cross-validation of the interviews contributes to the validity of the study, considering that the misinterpretation of the interviewee words from the interviewer could have occurred. Therefore, by validating in written their own thoughts, validity and credibility of the information given during the interview is confirmed.

3.6   Data Display

This represents an organized compilation of information which enables one to draw conclusions and take action. The researcher Data Display is presented in the Interview Appendix A, which also contains summaries of the interview for each individual respondent.

3.7   Conclusion Drawing/Verification

The researcher applied a Three-by-Three matrix (Prencipe et al., 2001) to categorize the information gained from the interviews (see Table 10). The horizontal dimension of the matrix refers to the processes: *experience accumulation, knowledge articulation and knowledge codification.* The vertical dimension refers to the level of analysis: individual, *project and organization.* From the interviews, the attempt was made to identify the mechanisms used for knowledge transfer and learning facilitation at individual, group and organization level. Accordingly, the processes the Case Company X utilizes in terms of experience accumulation, knowledge articulation and knowledge codification were identified. Each category of mechanisms for tacit and explicit knowledge was divided into columns, and the statements from the respondents were arranged and written down in the appropriate category (Table 10).

TABLE 10
THREE-BY-THREE MATRIX

| Level of analysis | Learning Processes | | |
	Experience Accumulation	Knowledge Articulation	Knowledge Codification
Individual	Mechanism statement of respondent(s)*	*	*
Project	*	*	*
Organizational/Company	*	*	*

41

*Source: Principe and Tell, 2001 * The statements concerning each of the mechanisms for tacit and explicit knowledge were written down when the interviews were analyzed.*

The analysis of the typology of the learning mechanisms used for each category of knowledge (i.e. tacit and explicit) as well as the analysis of vertical and horizontal dimensions enabled the researcher to create a picture of the learning landscape that characterized Case Company X. Thereafter, gained findings were used as a basis for recommendations made for answering the research question: *"How can knowledge transfer be increased and learning improved in and between projects at Case Company X in UK?"*

3.8   Reliability of Data

The validity and reliability of a qualitative research depends on the information collecting instruments. Apart from the intuitive meaning, reliability measures the extent to which a concept delivers the same results no matter how many times it is applied (Bryman et al., 2003). It has to do with consistency in results of the measuring device/instrument. If the answers from respondents form a pattern of similarity, then reliability is present. The researcher conducted seven interviews and the respondents gave answers which were similar in pattern. Therefore, the researcher claims the study to be reliable and feels that the study would be the same if it was conducted again in the future with other respondents within the programme division at Case Company X.

3.9   Validity of Data

Validity is the degree to which the instrument is measuring what it is supposed to be measuring. In the qualitative research, validity is ensured by getting access to the best possible informants.

Guba & Lincoln (1994) have proposed four criteria to judge the soundness of qualitative research, presented below:
- Credibility;
- Transferability;
- Dependability; and
- Confirmability.

Credibility – the results of the qualitative research are credible or believable from the perspective of the respondents (i.e. participants) in the research. Considering that the situation of interest for the participants has been addressed, the results of the research can be considered credible from the researcher's point of view. Credibility was insured also by the 'triangulation' of data.

Transferability- represents the degree to which the results can be generalized or transferred to other contexts or settings. The researcher has done a detailed job of describing the research context, therefore has ensured transferability being possible.

Dependability – emphasizes the need for the researcher to account for changing context that occurs during the research. Considering that there were no changes applicable, there was no need to account for a changing context.

Confirmability – represents the degree to which results could be confirmed by others. The researcher has conducted a data audit, by examining the data procedures and collection and eliminated the potential bias as much as possible. The interviews were sent to the interviewees.

The researcher has answered the research question and fulfilled her purpose of the study. The answer is presented in the conclusion chapter. Regarding the interview manual, it was based on literature review consisting of recent theories within the knowledge sharing and transfer and learning field which was the goal to be studied and analyzed by the researcher.

The methodology chapter expanded on the philosophy, approach and strategy used in this study. Moreover, the data collection approach was elaborated, ensuring validity and reliability criteria is fulfilled. In the next chapter, the analysis of the data will be presented, based on the three-by-three matrix mentioned in the verification section.

4.   ANALYSIS OF DATA

This chapter presents the data analysis of the researcher, and it illustrates the approaches of Case Company X to managing knowledge and the main mechanisms (i.e. for tacit and explicit knowledge) adopted.   The information considering the categories of tacit and explicit knowledge are extracted from the interviews and analyzed, as well as the processes and environment they co-exist in.

The researcher has used the Three-by-Three matrix (Prencipe et al., 2001) to extract information from the interviews relevant to the identified categories in the literature review. The researcher found it important to emphasize the processes used in knowledge management and transfer, and the enviroment that promotes it.   From the reviewed literature the categories of tacit, explicit and processes was established but when reviewing the empirical data the researcher saw the need to look at these categories in relation to what learning landscape they create and co-exist with.   The concept of learning landscape takes into account the multidimensional character of a company's approach to managing knowledge and learning (Prencipe et al., 2001).   The researcher did not develop a performance measure to assess the effectiveness of the different mechanisms adopted by the firm for project learning and knowledge transfer.

The three identified types of learning landscapes are:

- The explorer (*or L-shaped*) landscape: Companies rely on people-embedded knowledge, and emphasize experience accumulation process and knowledge transfer through people-to-people communication, and are characterized by a strong and friendly culture.
- The navigator (*or T-shaped*) landscape: Companies start to implement mechanisms for project learning based on a knowledge articulation process.   The mechanisms are implemented at individual, project and especially at organizational/company level.
- The exploiter (*or staircase)* landscape: Companies are already involved in the advance development of Information Technology based tools to support their project learning.   They deliberately attempt to codify and store knowledge developed during the execution of a project and document it so that it becomes easier to be accessed and exploited for the rest of the project and organization/company members (pp. 15-20).

In order to provide any relevant recommendations for knowledge transfer increase and improved learning in Case Company X, the company learning landscape needed to be elaborated and understood. Analyzing the learning mechanisms, the processes and the way they are utilized as well as the environment they co-exist enabled us to understand the Case Company X way of operating. When all the interviews had been conducted, the data were elaborated and this enabled the identification and evaluation of a pattern which emerged in the context of a learning landscape. When a picture of learning "landscape" was established, the researcher wanted to identify the reason which could explain why the learning "landscape" looked the way it did. If the current mechanisms and landscape was not contributing to knowledge transfer and learning in Case Company X, the recommendations given by the researcher should give alternatives on how to deal with the problems identified and how to solve them.

The Three-by-Three matrix (Prencipe et al., 2001) with the listed empirical data is shown in Table 11. Moreover, the data is presented in terms of mechanisms (i.e. for tacit and explicit knowledge) used in individual, project or organizational level and the learning process they relate to. Also, a contribution of the learning climate and environment of Case Company X towards learning and knowledge transfer is analyzed.

4.1   Findings in empirical data

The Three-by-Three Matrix (see Table 11) containing the researcher's empirical data is shown bellow followed by summations of the results based on the frequency of usage of each mechanism mentioned by the interviewees. The initiatives activated to stimulate knowledge transfer were many, and they will be presented in context of the processes. In addition, the company's culture embedded will be analyzed with the Schein model (Schein, 1992).

TABLE 11
THREE-BY-THREE MATRIX OF COMPANY X IN UK

Level of analysis	Learning Processes		
	Experience Accumulation	Knowledge Articulation	Knowledge Codification
Individual	On-the-job training/briefings Job rotation Coaching Mentoring Re-use of personnel/experts Shadowing	Notes Performance Appraisal Systems	Individual System Design Self-Designed Reporting System
Project	Person-to-person communication Informal encounters Workshops Domain expertise	Brainstorming Phase reviews Critical project reviews Monthly Reviews Quarterly Reviews Meetings on PM experience De-briefing meetings – monthly on project and program level Ad-hoc meetings	Project Management Plan(s) Milestones/Deadlines Action and Decision Logs Project history files Central Database repository Lessons learned Database Project Manuals

Organizational/Company		
Informal company routines, rules, guidelines and selection processes	Intra-project correspondence	Knowledge Maps (Company Road Map)
	Lessons learned	
	Succession Sessions	
	Competence Framework	
Review Committee(s)	Knowledge Inventory	Programme Development and Finance Organization (PDFO)
Risk Panel	Inter-project meetings	Project Management Office (PMOs)
Programme boards	Professional Networks	Process Description/Flowcharts – processes
Retreat (Away Days)	Coaching for Performance	XY training school
Simulations	Research project/dissertation	Web-portal
Career Development Opportunity Exchange (CDOX)		

4.2.1 Experience Accumulation process

As mentioned above the mechanisms that were identified were presented specifically in individual, project and company/organization context. A detailed description of each is presented in the text below.

Individual level: *the mechanisms identified were on job training (OJT), job rotation, coaching, mentoring, re-usage of personnel, and shadowing.*

On Job Training
Case Company X practices on job training because it believes it's more effective. The whole idea behind it is to get the job done and being instructed by their peers. Practicing hands on project management is considered to be the best way to learn and share knowledge. Direct experience of a particular practice is seen as most effective way of getting a feel for project activities.

Job rotation
Case Company X assigns staff to different activities (i.e. projects) as a way of broadening and extending their experience. Developing employees with a broad experience of different areas has advantage of flexibility. This enables the company to allocate their staff more easily to different projects. Key project roles are based on a multiple points of contact and overlapping set of skills. Job rotation idea is also to minimize the disruption caused by departure of particular individuals.

Coaching
Coaching practices are present in Case Company X, wherein the focus is on performance (i.e. job performance) and there is a specific agenda. And coaching has line management responsibility. It tries to focus on improvement of behavior of personnel in Case Company X. Because the coach has a level of authority (implicit or explicit) there is a compliance requirement within Case Company X.

Mentoring
Informal mentoring practices are in existence and were confirmed by all the interviewees. In this case the focus is the individual and there is no pre-set agenda and it is perceived as a two-way mutual beneficial relationship, with a power free environment. In some cases these practices are formalized by making mentoring an expected activity which is reviewed in staff

appraisals. Nevertheless, Case Company X applies mentoring because it is considered a knowledge and experience sharing initiative using a self-discovery approach of the individual.

Re-usage of personnel

Case Company X attempts to keep the same teams of people working on similar projects so that experience is directly transferred. In this way the experience is used more systematically in the setting up and execution of subsequent projects. There are differences in opinion on the continuity issue. For some project managers such continuity is an ideal but it is not always practical to achieve, considering that people will relevant experience may not be available.

Training

Even though they prefer OJT this does not mean that formal training is not worthwhile, and Case Company X invests resources in training its employees. Case Company X is considered one of the best for training, as the interviewees emphasized, if there is a training need identified for their personnel Case Company X will provide it. Formal training accelerates learning by drawing on the collected experience of those involved in the activity, but what is learned does not become relevant until it is applied. The training needs are identified on individual basis, and then the focus is on best method for achieving the training outcome. Case Company X considers it a responsibility of the manager and the employee to ensure that the correct training is being employed at the right time and with the appropriate support to facilitate the learning. The training provided by Case Company X is computer based training (CBT), Internal Training(s) and External Training(s) provided by APM.

Shadowing

Shadowing is an informal opportunity to learn from watching someone else in a particular role. Case Company X considers it particularly useful for individuals within Programmes to see an expert at work at a given task or using a particular behavior.

Project level: *the mechanisms identified were person-to-person communications, informal encounters, workshops and domain expertise.*

Person-to-person communication

Case Company X applies informal project reviews, the project manager and other team members can call these reviews on specific issues. Inter project informal reviews are held in the form of staff meetings between all project managers. As a consequence of this there is an informal network of project managers created. Some PM's practice one-to-one meetings with their team members in order to receive the latest updates on the projects as well as to get feedback on the degree of satisfaction of the team member with the environment he is working in.

Informal encounters
Case Company X applies informal encounters between PMs and also with PgMs. Programme managers provide their full support and express the benefits of knowledge transfer. Also, there is an open-minded attitude for suggesting new initiatives for knowledge transfer enhancement.

Workshops
Informal ways of knowledge sharing have been institutionalized via seminars and workshops given by speakers on specific (usually technical) subjects. Externally, considering that Case Company X is a paid member of Major Projects Association (MPA), the attendance to seminars is free of charge for Case Company X personnel.

Domain expertise
They have domain expertise, for example supply chain management. If a person has never experienced working with suppliers, they can go and be advised and have sessions with the suppliers, therefore enabling transfer of their knowledge and their expertise to the person requesting it.

Organizational/Company level: *mechanisms identified were informal company guidelines and rules, review committees, risk panel, programme boards, retreats (away days), simulations, and career development opportunity exchange (CDOX).*

Review Committees
There are different types of review committees established for different purposes. They are: Lessons Learned Review Committee (LLRC), long term projects review committee, development committee, phase review committee, critical project review committee, etc. In order to avoid redundancy of information a committee is established which review the MRI's every six weeks and decide which are the relevant 'lessons learned' to be kept in the system.

LLRC gets together on bimonthly basis, and they are in charge of filtering, retaining and publishing the necessary information. The participants of LLRC have different backgrounds which gives it more credibility. There are three actions that come out of the lessons learned review in terms of the projects and processes and that is (i) change the process, (ii) improve the project and/or (iii) take no action- data storing.

Risk Panel
Is established to analyze the content of Risk Analysis and Management Plan reports, and review the necessary material which needs to be kept in the system.

Programme boards
There are different types of boards within Case Company X, and their existence is justified by authorizing budget changes and project/programme scope changes. They are the mechanism for change within projects and programmes. They lead the change that occurs in Case Company X. Board sets the milestones which need to be realized. Therefore, the staff is fully committed to the realization of the milestones and Case Company X has had an excellent track record on milestone achievement. The Strategy and Policy Boards hold meetings on quarterly basis, whereas Performance Review Boards hold meetings on monthly basis.

Retreat (Away days)
There are retreats of away days organized three times a year, with an overnight duration, held outside the company facilities. This is done with the goal of sharing experience and discussing on current projects within programmes.

Simulations
Within the training Case Company X utilizes simulations which enable people to acquire skills required. Simulations are beneficial because they create an artificial environment wherein people learn how to react to tasks, and make mistakes and learn from them. The positive step is that there are no repercussions if mistakes are made during simulations.

Career Development Opportunity Exchange (CDOX)
The Career Development Opportunity Exchange or CDOX is an on-line tool applied by Case Company X, wherein short term development opportunities can be made known by those able to offer them and found by those looking for them. The tool is used to advertise short term development opportunities – something where help is needed or a particular experience that would offer an opportunity for someone else to broaden their experience. It is also used by staff to look for short term development opportunities.

4.2.2 Knowledge Articulation Process

Individual level: _mechanisms identified were notes, performance appraisal systems._

Notes
Some of the PM in Case Company X produce their own notes containing 5 key lessons learned which need to be presented in the monthly project meeting.

Performance appraisal systems
Case Company X conducts a performance appraisal for its personnel, but it is mostly related to team collaboration and behaviors. There is no specific section referring to contribution to knowledge sharing and knowledge transfer.

Project level: _mechanisms identified were brainstorming, project reviews, and meetings on project management experiences, intra-project correspondence, lessons learned, succession sessions and competency framework._

Project reviews
The company has institutionalized a number of different types of project reviews that are embedded and formalized in the business process. The formal reviews can be categorized in two main groups. (1) reviews led by auditors external to the process, the aim of these reviews is to assess performance status, risks, costs, schedule of the project and lessons learned from previous projects. The diffusion of the outcome of these reviews is limited to those responsible for conducting the reviews and to the corporate managers who assess the project's merits. (2) reviews led by a project team member (usually the project manager) , they are project reviews held on monthly basis, which are software, design, customer, quality reviews. The outcomes of these reviews are documented and stored electronically and are available to project members and the reports produced are in the database available to wider audience.

Specifically, Case Company X conducts four types of reviews: phase reviews, critical project reviews, monthly reviews and quarterly reviews.

Phase reviews are conducted during the project, with the goal of assessing the progress, risks, plans and business case. Phase review enables the company to check the project progress, ensuring that it is on track and supported by the senior management. The phase review process provides a structure for the review meetings, produces formal results, and issues Phased Review Certificates. Regarding the process, it is usually decided at project inception if there is a need for a phase review, and accordingly it ensures that the Project Manager conducts the review. A team of Assessors – experienced and independent employees- are appointed, in order to provide the valuable independent feedback. Nevertheless, PM is responsible for providing all the information asked by assessors, and is the administrator of the Phase Review Process. Accordingly, a Go recommendation (symbolized with green color), a Go with reservation recommendation (amber), or a No-Go recommendation (red) is given. When Go with reservation is recommended, a corrective action needs to be taken immediately and retained and documented in the projects MRI. Review meetings contribute to the explicit knowledge codification, by being recorded in MRI and filed accordingly. A formal result produced by phase review is that they are registered in the database of the company, and are supposed to be utilized and referred to in the future projects. Furthermore, an annual report is produced containing the main findings on the selected projects for the phased review, improvements to the process and any general lessons to be learnt. The Phased Review Certificates are also stored in the Project MRI and are evaluated bi-annually.

Critical project review is conducted across all the selected projects at least once every 8 weeks. A process is also set up, leaded by a team of two independent reviewers and a representative from the finance department. A formal result produced by critical project reviews is the reports which are uploaded in the database of the company, and are usually utilized and referred to in the future projects. Monthly reviews which are done more at the programme level, wherein opportunities for process improvement are identified and followed-up. And the quarterly reviews are also conducted at higher instances from the programme(s) division board members.

Meetings on project management experiences
Are organized on weekly basis, wherein the project manager meets with the programme manager to discuss and reflect upon their experience on project management of past week. The experience should have value to add to others.

Meetings on project progress
The frequency of meetings depends on project duration. Some PM hold meetings on weekly basis, but the minimum requirement is for meetings to be held on monthly basis. Nevertheless, if there is an urgent matter, extraordinary meetings- ad-hoc meetings- are called upon. Sometimes meetings take form of teleconferences considering the movement factor of people in the team. All the projects have guidelines for conducting the meetings, which agenda is based on the framework of Terms of Reference of the project. The minutes

of the meetings in some cases are sent as a summary through email to all the participants, but not all programmes practice it. However, the tangible outputs of the meetings are the Actions and Decision Logs which are recorded to the project and programme MRI. The tangible outputs are compulsory for all projects. Also, electronic copies of the templates used in the meetings are held in the database for a period of minimum one year.

Intra-project correspondence
The templates for project correspondence are designed and updated and improved on continual basis from the PDFO. The templates are there for all the mechanisms and the processes, naming few: change requests, project status reports, and lessons learned report, phase review report, critical project review report, monthly review report, project closure report etc.

Lessons learned
Lessons learned are a result of different types of reviews and are stored in the specific lessons learned database, which link is in the Intranet. Case Company X had a lessons learned process for a long time, but it was in the lessons learned exercise format. This exercise was conducted only at the end of the project, and the outcome was a written report. The report would not always be stored in the database and reference was not made to future projects. Therefore, Case Company X decided to change the process by updating a lessons learned process and establishing the lessons learned database and review committee. Lessons learned are encouraged to be produced at the end of each phase of the project as well as at the end of the project. Lessons learned database is organized if four broad categories: costs, people, process and procedures. There was a noticeable discrepancy between if the lessons learned are a compulsory requirement or not.

Succession sessions
The succession sessions are conducted frequently and the goal is to identify the person that can replace or succeed another person within the project or in between projects if the person departs on short notice. This is a contingency strategy to minimize the knowledge loss.

Competence framework
It is being developed by Case Company X, which provides a tool for knowledge identification and identification of people training needs. Case Company X has identified the need to apply a competency framework as a part of continuing professional development of its personnel. The competency framework will be based on the framework designed by the APM; nevertheless, it will contain a smaller and more generalized number of competences to be assessed on individual level.

mechanisms identified were knowledge inventory, knowledge facilitators and managers, inter-project meetings, inter-project correspondence, professional networks, sessions on knowledge transfer, coaching for performance and initiation and participation in the research project/dissertation.

Knowledge inventory
Case Company X has work centers from where they get the people with the required skills for the project. The database provides a skill set for all the project team members, so that everyone has knowledge of people if they need a specific skill. Nevertheless, the database for people skills is not updated frequently enough.

Inter-project meetings
Once in a month project managers participate in meetings with a group of managers and senior programme manager of the specific programme. The goal of the meeting is to inform the senior programme manager on the status of the active project, or more projects considering that they can run more than on project simultaneously. Project Manager(s) need to prepare for these meetings considering the amount of questions to be asked by top management. In order to avoid surprises, the agenda is set and sent to the project managers in advance so that they can prepare. The outcome of the meetings are recorded on actions and decisions logs. Additionally, the project managers got to know more about projects in the portfolio of the programme and company, in which they were not directly involved.

Professional networks
Top management encourages their staff to affiliate with professional bodies, focusing more on APM and MPA. Company X sends staff to be certified by APM, as well as many of Company X employees are sent to seminars organized by the professional bodies, some of them being guess speakers especially the senior programme managers. The aim is to encourage PM(s) to focus on new achievements in project management and to search for inspiration outside the company. Furthermore, it enhances the establishment of a shared frame of reference and increases the possibilities for successful communication. Case Company X funds training for its staff which is organized by the professional bodies.

Coaching for performance
It is a career development opportunity designed by Case Company X. It enables staff within Case Company X to relocate to other projects or programmes. The opportunities for a

different job experience are published in the web-portal, with the details on the job description and the required skills. The participation can be from 1 day to six months to longer period.

Initiation and participation in the research project/dissertation
Initiation and funding for a master student to conduct a research project/dissertation was another way of top management trying to emphasize and strive for knowledge transfer. Allocation of time to participate in the research created opportunities the project management personnel to reflect upon and discuss the knowledge issue. All the respondents were eager to discuss knowledge transfer in the dialogues and research meetings.

4.2.3 Knowledge Codification process

Individual level: *mechanisms identified were individual system design and self-designed reporting system.*

Individual system design
Some of the projects considering the dissatisfaction with the central repository database have decided to set up a structure specific for their programme.

Self designed reporting system
PM sometimes develop their own reporting system, wherein they ask their staff members to prepare in advance for the questions and for example submit key lessons learned before the weekly or monthly meetings.

Project level: *mechanisms identified were project management plans, milestones/deadlines, actions and decisions logs, project history files, lessons learned database, web-portal, central database repositories , project certificates, project manuals, project improvement plans.*

Actions and decisions logs
The outcomes of the meetings are recorded in actions and decisions logs of the project. It is compulsory for all projects to follow up on the actions wherein a target date to clear the action(s) is set. Also the decisions undertaken are recorded for future reference.

Project history files
The (MRI) containing all the technical information is stored in the database. The MRI is a requirement for each project and can be used for future reference.

Central database repository
All the projects have the database with the file structure and lessons learned templates as methods for capturing explicit knowledge. The technical reports otherwise called the MRI for each project are stored in the database. Case Company X grants the access to the database to all the members of the different project teams. Nevertheless, Case Company X reliance is mostly based on the data and strict documentation rules, by utilizing the templates and the different reporting formats. Database used at Case Company X is not so user-friendly but it is a common denominator for project work in the company, representing a substantial resource for all the projects, small or large. Project team members are trained in using it, and are updated if there are any changes. It is important to note that the templates are uploaded in the database from the International Technology experts; therefore, there is no need for project members to upload any reports, just to give their input directly in the database. This enables them to save on time, which would normally be lost uploading the different files, which would create conflict in the prioritization process of the files and reports.

Lessons learned has a specific database centralizing all the lessons learned reports of all the projects across all programmes. Considering that it is a new website, it has not been tested enough to consider its benefit. Nevertheless, the usage of the database has increased and there are statistics being recorded on continual basis. However, the database needs to be publicized at all instances so that its usage is increased and its benefit is realized.

Organizational/Company level: *mechanisms identified were knowledge maps- Case Company X road map, programme development and financial organization (PDFO), project management office(s), processes and their description (i.e. through flowcharts), annual reports, progress report templates at programme level, programme history file (MRI), XYZ training school and Web-Portal.*

Case Company X road map
In 2004 Case Company X has reviewed its project management capability and got a result that was not pleasing for a company that wanted to be world class in project management. Therefore, they established a capability maturity model (road map) and have since been moving forward at an accelerating speed and have reached level 4 (i.e. total of 5 levels). This was made possible through development and improvement in processes and mechanisms.

Programme Development and Financial Organization (PDFO)
Top management decided to establish an organizational unit for project management as a knowledge sharing initiative. The unit was established to emphasize the striving for more

professional project management. PDFO ensures that regular process reviews are undertaken and project performance is reviewed. The outputs are the development of project improvement plans and objectives from evaluated results. It plays a vital role in aiding communication, prioritization and integration across projects.

Project Management Office(s)
At a programme level a PMO office is established to manage multiple projects at organizational level, but also as a knowledge sharing initiative. The PMO is there to ensure successful implementation of projects through the availability of predictable and re-usable tools, techniques and processes. They usually consolidate and distribute data therefore contributing to knowledge transfer. In addition, the PMO ensures training in project management skills. Also PMO reviews the reports produced and decides which ones should be kept in the system for future reference.

Processes and their description
The processes are part of the governance set of Case Company X, and their description is done through flowcharts. The process description is guidance for the person using it, and in the beginning of the project they are presented to the project team members. Even though they are not very user-friendly they still add value to the project execution and lead to project completion. Nevertheless, processes do not make up for performance. The processes have been improved in the recent years, but the time used to fill paper work for processes can be used for more value adding activities. A review cycle is done every two years wherein all the processes are reviewed, and the process owner can decide based on the feedback received if the change needs to be made.

XY Training School
It is a sub-programme within one of the major Programmes. It is a knowledge sharing initiative dedicated to training and refresh training of Case Company X personnel. In addition, they provide training for outside overseas parties. X training school introduces the latest tools to be used in the company, and trains personnel of their usage. The name of the school cannot be disclosed for commercially sensitive reasons.

Web-portal
The critical issues arising are published in the intranet, the web-portal of the company, made available for wider audience. The publication on the intranet depends on the criticality of the work and the issue at stake.

4.3 Culture perspective on knowledge transfer

Schein(1992) has developed a framework to represent knowledge transfer in the cultural perspective context. Moreover, he emphasized the importance of cultural changes being supported by primary culture-embedding mechanisms and secondary articulation and reinforcement mechanisms (Schein, 1992) (See Table 12).

TABLE 12
CULTURE EMBEDDING AND ARTICULATION/REINFORCMENT MECHANISMS IN
COMPANY X IN UK

	Creating arenas for knowledge transfer	Giving top management attention	Organizational design	Organizational systems and procedures	Design of physical space	Organizational rites and rituals
Shared office					✓	
On Job Training	✓					✓
Job Rotation	✓		✓		✓	
Coaching	✓	✓		✓		
Training	✓	✓		✓		
Shadowing	✓					✓
Person-to- person communication	✓	✓				✓
Informal reviews	✓					✓
Review Committees	✓	✓		✓		
Programme Boards	✓	✓		✓		
Retreats	✓					✓
Simulations	✓	✓		✓		
Career Development Opportunity Exchange	✓	✓		✓		
Performance Appraisal Systems	✓	✓		✓		

Project Reviews	✓	✓		✓	✓
De-briefing meetings - monthly on project and program level	✓	✓		✓	
Lessons learned	✓	✓		✓	
Succession Sessions	✓	✓			✓
Competence Framework	✓	✓		✓	
PM as reporters	✓				
Knowledge Inventory	✓		✓		✓
APM communities of practice	✓	✓			✓
Coaching for performance	✓	✓	✓		✓
Participation in research project	✓	✓			
Self Designed reporting system	✓				✓
Project History Files (MRI)	✓	✓		✓	
Central Database – repository	✓	✓		✓	
Actions and Decisions Log	✓	✓		✓	
Lessons learned database	✓	✓		✓	
Case Company X roadmap	✓	✓		✓	
PDFO	✓	✓	✓	✓	
Project Management Office	✓	✓	✓		
Processes	✓	✓		✓	
Training School	✓	✓	✓	✓	
Web-Portal	✓	✓		✓	

Source: Schein, 1992

All the respondents acknowledge Case Company X implementing continuous latest mechanisms and processes to improve the knowledge sharing and transfer, because they believe it impacts greatly the projects performance. This can be seen with the number of mechanisms that are applied for sharing knowledge and experience, and they are implemented and updated on continuous basis. Case Company X considers their personnel as an important asset; therefore continuous professional development is considered a cornerstone for Case Company X life. It is a process which keeps the Case Company X personnel motivated and interested in their work, and represents a drive to progress in their careers.

We can see from Table 12 that Case Company X provides an arena for knowledge transfer and knowledge creation. Moreover, the top management is aware of the striving towards creating a knowledge transfer environment and they are regularly updated on the latest initiatives. Organizational design does not greatly affect the knowledge transfer considering that most of the mechanisms do not fall in the respective category. The systems and procedures within Case Company X are already put in place, therefore, the lack of systems cannot be considered the reason for sometimes failing to share the knowledge and more importantly not learn from mistakes. Case Company X has implemented an open office as a design from physical space, wherein, project personnel with different responsibilities and titles are located in the same office area, in order to eliminate the feeling of power and distance. And finally, there are company rituals and rites present within Case Company X which facilitate knowledge sharing and transfer.

Nevertheless, considering that it has become a result oriented culture, the feeling is present that when a project is undertaken, personal or divisional success becomes the most important factor, and not the goal of achieving the best result for the benefit of the company as a whole. The PMs respect each others working style and they try not to intervene in each others business. Sometimes the feeling is present that other people's time is wasted if there are visits made to ask for inquiries which for some people are considered needless. Moreover, it does not instill a no-blame culture considering that people are held accountable for their actions. Due to existence of the following factors, the PMs are prevented from a deeper and intensive knowledge transfer, even though they are willing to participate in knowledge transfer. As stated by Schein (1992) knowledge transfer needs to be consistent with the prevalent cultural values and the basic underlying assumptions.

4.4   Empirical findings in relation to the research propositions

As emphasized during the study, the research found that the mechanisms for transferring of tacit and explicit knowledge are common denominators in the literature. Moreover the processes and the company environment they co-exist are proven to play a crucial role and impact the knowledge transfer greatly. Based on these divisions, an attempt is made to elaborate on how knowledge transfer and learning is achieved in a learning organization.

The researcher, based on the developed research categories, has studied how these categories are present at Case Company X. Moreover, the categories have been discussed and elaborated in the context of empirical data collected, which enabled the creation of a learning landscape at Case Company X.

Based on the findings, Case Company X is considered to pertain to the "*The exploiter (or staircase) landscape*", because it has already been involved in the advance development of Information Communication Technology (ICT) mechanisms to support knowledge transfer and learning. They mainly codify and store knowledge in report formats in the database so that it is easy accessed and utilized by the company and its programme division.

The findings above support the identified propositions. As it can be seen from Table 11 and 12, there is clear evidence that Case Company X has embedded significant amount of mechanisms with the purpose of increasing knowledge transfer and improving learning within its programme division. Also processes are already being implemented. Moreover, the environment the company implements is impacting the knowledge transfer and learning. Nevertheless, some of the practices applied by Case Company X are different from what the literature is proposing. Therefore, a number of suggestions will be discussed in the next chapter and a number of recommendations will be provided in the conclusion chapter for Case Company X.

5.   DISCUSSION

The findings in the empirical data give an overview of the learning 'landscape' at Case Company X. The detailed representation of data is provided in Three-by-Three matrix (Table 11). The researcher will discuss how Case Company X promotes knowledge transfer and learning and propose recommendation to the problems they face, all based on the literature reviewed. The data presented are collected from secondary sources such as governance policies and guidelines of Case Company X, and primary inputs from the industry practitioners (i.e. interviews conducted, see Appendix A).

5.1   Project based learning in and between projects

As mentioned in the literature review chapter the goal of project based learning is to define the process of creating, sharing, distributing, capturing and understanding knowledge in a company. It is considered crucial and important to have an effective knowledge management. This is supported by research done by Karlsen & Gottschalk (2004) which shows that effective knowledge management reduces errors and repetition of mistakes, decreases the unnecessary workload, improves services, enhances profitability and produces better decisions and solutions. Having a more active knowledge management (as in Case Company X) will give companies a competitive advantage, as supported by Ayas (1996).

Even though the vision of knowledge management is spoken in Case Company X, there is limited effectiveness in its conduction at company level, especially in the process of organizational learning. Therefore, the "Phased Model Approach to Intra organizational Learning", proposed by Harvey et al., (1998) can be applied at Case Company X, to further enhance learning and knowledge transfer:
*   Stimulate learning between management levels in the organization;
*   Expansion of learning environment across functions;
*   Encourage learning between divisions within the same company; and
*   Bolster learning between organizations within a single company (pp. 345-347).

When prompted to reflect on and explain how Case Company X generally sourced new knowledge, reflected on issues and how they intervened in the learning situations they participated in, their responses reflected their ease and understanding and promotion of this topic. This was demonstrated through their direct responses to the questions, and illustrated with practical examples conducted within Case Company X. It was clear that there was an ownership of the project, its goals and its processes and also implanted the notion of a constantly learning and changing organization in all levels of the hierarchy as advocated by Sense (2008).

During the interviews, it was clear that the roles and responsibilities were assigned in advance, and they had clarity on how exactly to conduct their activities to achieve their goals for the project. As concluded by Müller (2009, p.2), governance provides a clear distinction between *ownership* and *control* of tasks. Moreover, there were formal processes for them to grasp onto and apply to aid their achievement of the challenging project tasks. The fact that the project participants had information and guidance on the processes at the start of the project, contributed to a build up of their confidence and authority and investigate more deeply the project learning opportunities. This is also supported by Hameri et al., (1998) who emphasize the need for clear definitions and well-documented processes to be adopted by project based companies.

Governance is a need and represents a fact of life for Case Company X. With governance they ensure that the project maps on to the strategic objectives, the basis of funding decisions and the basis of resource allocation. Governance is achieved through the PDFO as well as the locally assigned PMO(s) within each programme. At a programme level a PMO office is established to manage multiple projects at organizational level, but also as a knowledge sharing initiative. The establishment of PMO and PDFO is encouraged by APM (2004).

Nevertheless, there are also difficulties which Case Company X faces. One of them was the high time pressure on the project managers and their team during the project as well as upon project completion. This prevents them from dedicating more time to production of more qualitative lessons learned reports and knowledge transfer. The fear of negative sanctions if mistakes are made is present in Case Company X. The reason why they don't promote a no-blame and no-mistakes culture is because they hold project personnel accountable for their actions and their results. Some team members do not see the usage of coding experience; therefore they do not spend time on knowledge creation and accumulation. The input of senior management is of crucial importance for knowledge sharing, but as the interviewees said, the best people are always busy. All these factors have been identified by Schindler et al., (2003) .

The empirical evidence revealed that the company uses a combination of formal and informal mechanisms for knowledge transfer and learning and the two types of mechanisms are complementary in use. According to APM (2006, p.116) *"formal and informal networks offer the opportunity to share experience, tacit knowledge and lessons learned."* The mechanisms are applied through the processes, and the environment they co-exist in plays a crucial role.

5.2   Tacit knowledge

It is clear that Case Company X has a sustainable number of mechanisms to capture tacit knowledge. There were deliberate attempts made to "select" successful routines and practices and carry them forward into subsequent projects. Project capability was built from a 'top down' approach, and new company specific routines, processes and ICT tools were developed to execute a growing volume of projects more efficiently and effectively.

Case Company X has a much lower level of staff turnover (i.e. 5%) compared to other companies in UK, as based on the interviewees. They create a working environment wherein project team members are satisfied and are willing to share their knowledge. This is in line with Mumford (1994) advocating that companies need to provide the right environment for knowledge transfer and learning.

Ayas (1996) recommends a shift in project management philosophy towards a knowledge creating structure. To achieve the shift, Case Company X's management needs to invest their resources towards educating their project managers on the importance and benefits of knowledge transfer and learning. Different measures like workshops and trainings were undertaken by Case Company X to educate their personnel.

Most of the respondents' perceive the company policy as one in which most of the time the best engineers and technicians are selected for Project Managers position. It seems that not always the best engineers can be the most suitable for project managers' positions. Therefore, Case Company X advocates not only technical/engineering competences, but also project management competences, importance being given to the "soft" skills. They have initiated the creation of a competency framework to evaluate the competences of their personnel. Competence framework has been advocated as a necessary framework by APM (2008).

The fact that work meetings are conducted on a regular basis contributes to tacit knowledge transfer. They are organized at a project level and a programme level. The need for conducting evaluation meetings more often to produce lessons learned information is emphasized by Kotnour (2000). Moreover, he states that it contributes to the success of the project and increases the performance.

In terms of human resources management approaches the researcher considered the following: selection, training and development, appraisal, and motivation. An aspect of selection is the continuity in staffing. This ensures the strategic transfer explained by Dixon (Dixon, 2000). Also, Case Company X people assigned to a specific task request information on the task by people who have already done it, therefore enabling strategic transfer. Moreover, there are tentatives to implement the expert transfer, by asking the senior project and programme managers, who are experts in their field, to share their experience with the junior people in the company. Considering that Case Company X outsource some of their services to experts, wherein the expert shares the knowledge with the persons involved in the project, this enables expert transfer (Dixon, 2000; Karlsen & Gottschalk, 2003).

APM (2006) advocated the establishment of a PMO as an infrastructure to promote communities of practice. Case Company X has established PMO's within each of their major programmes, and it is considered a knowledge sharing initiative. The knowledge is disseminated within different projects which are part of the specific programme within Case Company X. Moreover, Case Company X has created strong links with APM and PMA, by sending their personnel to workshops, seminars and lessons conducted by them.

An old hierarchical style of organizing project work is present at Case Company X. The layers of Project Planners, Project Managers, Program Managers and Senior Programme Managers are present, and the authorization for a change request of approval is time consuming and not very effective. The PNS – team structure with self-managing teams-proposed by Ayas (1996) can be an alternative to running the projects. This will develop a more information-based structure within Case Company X, which enables people's involvement and enhances the knowledge base.

Woo et al. (2004) has introduced the Dynamic Knowledge Map as a tool to share tacit knowledge. It is a web based navigator, which helps to locate the right people that posses the knowledge needed to rectify a problem or issue. The database of Case Company X can apply the knowledge navigator.

Ayas & Zenuik (2001) advocate that management within companies need to create a context which allows project members to question existing institutional norms (i.e. mechanisms, processes). Case Company X encourages their personnel to change and challenge their processes and mechanisms.

Except tacit knowledge mechanisms, Case Company X also has institutionalized the explicit knowledge mechanisms discussed below.

5.3 Explicit knowledge

According to Nonaka et al., (1995) the key to knowledge creation is to convert tacit knowledge into explicit knowledge. Accordingly, the necessity to make tacit knowledge explicit has been recognized and is emphasized as important at Case Company X. They have a well established information systems infrastructure, consisting of many mechanisms and processes which are used as effective tools to enhance intra- and inter-project learning and knowledge transfer. Considering the large extent of projects they run within their programmes, there are already routines established to make tacit knowledge explicit, which are present across all the projects run in the Case Company X.

The company already is involved in advanced development of ICT-based tools to support their project learning, and adopts most of the mechanisms that are recommended by the academic and the practitioners' world. And also, notwithstanding the temporary nature of the task performed by the project company, there are routines developed which define how to approach projects.

All the projects have the database with the file structure and lessons learned templates and meetings as methods for capturing explicit knowledge. Lessons learned are as a result of different project reviews conducted by Case Company X. Lessons learned concentrate not only on the success parts of the project but as well as on the negative parts, which are in line with Disteter's research (2002). Evaluation meetings are conducted during and at the end of the projects, as a result lessons learned are produced. Kotnour (2000) emphasizes this and he believes it increases the success and performance of projects.

A very simplistic approach to preparing and structuring the contents of lesson learned after the project is completed is the use of Micro Articles (Wilke, 1998). This method does not tie up many resources and it is easy to implement. Considering the extensive quantity of the lessons learned reports, this could be used as an alternative application for lessons learned to be applied by Case Company X to capture explicit knowledge. Most importantly, the method is not time consuming which is important considering that time is a conflicting resource for all the personnel involved in the programme division within Case Company X. Learning History presented by Schindler et al. (2003) can also be implemented; nevertheless, it requires investing more resources and deeper team involvement of project members. Its importance lies in that it is written by the team members, representing their tacit knowledge made explicit to be used for future similar projects. Clear definitions and well-documented processes are established, is in accordance with Hameri et al. (1998) recommendations.

As can be seen, Case Company X, in order to improve the quality of lessons learned is implementing the five main success factors stated by Schindler et al. (2003):

- Regularly capture the most important experiences directly after important milestones with the entire project team;
- Have an external, neutral moderator of the debriefing workshop (not to be done by project managers or other team members);
- Perform the lessons learned gathering graphically i.e. collecting and structuring the project experiences along a time line and provide a workshop documentation in a poster format visible for all staff involved;
- Ensure a collective, interactive evaluation and analysis of experiences made by individual team members;
- Strive to gain a commitment in the sense of action consequences from the gathered insights (p. 227).

The Dynamic Knowledge Map recommended by Woo et al. (2004), can be used for explicit knowledge at Case Company X. It facilitates not only learning between individuals, but also leads to documents, templates, and databases through these individuals.

As mentioned above in the explicit category, project de-briefing techniques can have a positive impact on present and future project successes, as emphasized by Brisby (1999). The phase reviews are conducted at the end of each phase of the project. Projects that are subject to phase reviews are of importance for Case Company X. The perception and understanding of the significance of each separate process/phase in the project is emphasized by Mumford (1994). Each phase review at Case Company X has a defined process and timeline to ensure that it is well managed and effective. Critical project reviews are conducted on regular basis by Case Company X, and the outcome is the report which is stored in the Case Company X database. Nevertheless, this review is more independent and therefore it is considered credible. APM (2006) advocates the application of different types of project reviews.

The database existing in Case Company X is a common denominator for project work, and it is considered a substantial resource for all the projects, no matter the magnitude. Database, as a technological application, is considered an aid to solve a problem, according to Prusak et al. (1998). Moreover, Hameri et al., (1998), concluded that database facilitates learning through visualization of the collected data. The access to the database has been granted to all the members of different project teams, but different members have different levels of access based on their job responsibility.

Although the company encourages informal ways of knowledge sharing via forums and staff meetings, the procedure-oriented culture permeates the company and is the major driver for organizational and project performance improvements. A leaner structure of the company can be applied in the future, in order to instill a no-blame culture and to promote to a greater extent knowledge transfer and learning. A decentralized knowledge management structure could be applied, as advocated by Bayer et al., (cited in Jennex, 2005).

Moreover, the tacit knowledge is converted into explicit knowledge through usage of processes, which are discussed below.

5.4   Processes

Most of the literature on knowledge management and capturing is characterized by the tendency to think that the cost of codification activities are justified by their outcomes rather than by the cognitive implications of the processes as such (Zollo & Winter, 2001). In the empirical findings reported in this study, in comparison to the researchers the project based company has seemed to focus its effort on outcomes as well as on the processes of codification in developing technical devices and organizational mechanisms for learning between projects.

The need for clear definitions and well-documented processes in projects is emphasized by Hameri et al., (1998). As it can be seen, Case Company X has established and institutionalized such processes. Case Company X is characterized by formal project management processes, wherein there are process development managers and owners, who are in charge of developing and maintaining the project management processes. Project management process is software based so that the project documentation is organized in the database. The workload per person is formalized and computer-based. The project process is structured in disciplined, measurable and repeatable phases. This is in line with the project management process given by APM Body of Knowledge (APM, 2006).

The properties of codified knowledge should thus predominate over those of articulated knowledge. The company believes that the articulation is an intermediate step in the codification of knowledge, which is proposed by Zollo et al., (2001). Based on the empirical investigation of Case Company X in its establishment of mechanisms for project learning the researcher observed that the process through which knowledge is accumulated into tacit, articulated and codified knowledge is highly complementary. Informal processes are sometimes important, some knowledge is really hard to codify, but articulation and codification seems to help Case Company X in their pursuit for better knowledge about why some projects succeed and others fail. Codification is encouraged by Koskinen et al., (2003), who advocate codification of knowledge and its transfer to the database, which can be accessed by different team members.

The company has developed a generic process framework that encompasses all its business processes. A corporate function labeled PDFO is in charge of developing, updating and documenting the company's generic business processes. The organizational procedures are a general road map that broadly defines "what to do". The description of processes is done through flowcharts. The emphasis is on the business and project processes.

Process improvement is understood as an important source of business performance improvement. Revisions and updates are accomplished with a top-down approach. The quality team also carries out the Root Cause Analyses of problems that emerge during the execution of a project. The project level policies and procedures are stored in the database with access dependent on the job description. This is in line with Brady et al., (2004), advocating deposition of the accumulated knowledge in the database of the company. Moreover, the knowledge accumulated not only contributes to the upgrading of the actual database, but also past knowledge is utilized to improve current and future projects, which is also supported by Lampel et al. (2008).

The mechanisms and processes co-exist in harmony or not depending on the environment created by the company, which is discussed below.

5.5   Company Environment

Case Company X has expressed a vision in the company concerning knowledge and learning, which makes the knowledge sharing and creation easier. According to Gilbert & Cordey-Hayes (1996), in order to achieve success in organizational development, emphasis needs to be given to the promotion of a learning culture. Case Company X management is considered to be responsible for effectively promoting a learning culture, and this responsibility is taken seriously. Senior management support and resources are important for underpinning knowledge management and learning within Case Company X.

The environment is considered open, customer and productivity oriented. There is a hierarchy, but it is rigid when needed and often fairly flat with an open-office, open-door collaborative way of working. There is a clear procedure in place, and it is that and the solid skills base that allows the constantly changing nature of the projects to be tamed and marshaled to meet the deadlines. Case Company X has the excellent mix of skills by getting the right people in the right places. Case Company X utilizes a task oriented and team-based mode of operation.

The project teams are cross-functional, drawn from the work centers, with varied experience and specialist skills. Behavioral characteristics also complement knowledge and experience. The company tries to maintain a careful balance between formal and informal tools for learning between projects. It implements advanced knowledge management tools and involves staff and creates ownership. Senior management provides support for implementation of such mechanisms and processes.

Sense (2007) argues for developing a social infrastructure which is practical and participant-oriented. Case Company X enables their PMs and project team members to express their opinion and participate. Moreover, project managers create an informal network of contacts by referring to other project managers or other team members and get access to their knowledge. Even though Case Company X creates an environment wherein team members are empowered which is advocated by Kotnour (2000), it does not instill a no-blame culture as advocated by Brady et al., (2003). The fostering of a culture of frank disclosure of information and mistakes is also encouraged by APM (2006). In Case Company X, people are held responsible and accountable for their actions. Nevertheless, Case Company X encourages a culture where asking difficult questions and posing challenges are appreciated, as advocated by Pritchard (Pritchard, cited by APM, 2008).

Appraisal is based more on behavior and team work competences and not on knowledge transfer specifically. Interestingly, in the company there was no evidence of direct incentives (i.e. monetary benefits) associated with knowledge transfer. Rather, the codification of knowledge into reports, minutes, and lessons learned, etc. is based on a presumption of good behavior among members in the organization. An appropriate incentive scheme is promoted and encouraged by Brady et al. (2003).

Culture embedding mechanisms and articulation/reinforcement mechanisms are advocated by Schein (1992). The empirical results of the mechanisms adapted by Case Company X support the creation of arenas for knowledge transfer. Top management attention is engaged in knowledge transfer and learning, and the latest mechanisms and processes are attempted to be implemented on continuous basis at Case Company X.

As advocated by Sense (2008), if there is feeling of higher authority present, it impacts negatively the ability of people to learn effectively. Case Company X, in order to overcome this issue, has instilled a shared office, wherein all the levels of hierarchy share the same space. In addition, specific rituals and rites are within Case Company X which promotes knowledge sharing and transfer. They take more the form of informal meetings and encounters.

The above sections concerning tacit and explicit knowledge, processes and environment have reviewed the types of mechanisms, processes and environment as they co-exist in at Case Company X. The tools and techniques identified in the literature review have been associated to the specific categories mentioned above, in order to show possible improvements to the existing processes, mechanisms and environment as well as to provide solutions to problems if identified. The emphasis on particular mechanisms and processes applied by Case Company X, based on the Three-by-Three matrix has been presented and elaborated upon.

The suggestions from the reviewed literature will contribute to solve the problems identified and discussed in this chapter. Moreover, the conclusion and recommendation which will follow in the next chapter, the researcher will attempt to solve the underlying situation and issues. This will facilitate an answer to the research question of this study conducted.

6.   CONCLUSIONS

Based on the case study examined, this study has explored the knowledge transfer and learning by analyzing Company X. Knowledge transfer in and between projects in Company X seems to be an attractive goal for project managers, but it requires knowledge transfer and learning initiatives. The limited extent of this study and its focus on only projects within company X limits the generalizability of the researcher's findings. There is research needed to be done in the other divisions within Case Company X, for example Engineering Division.

The researcher's conclusions according to the research layout are presented. An extensive amount of literature was reviewed by the researcher in order to answer the research question: "*How can knowledge transfer be increased and learning improved in and between projects at Case Company X in UK?*". The clear answer to the research question was not visible after the data was reviewed. However, the researcher has identified the mechanisms; processes and environment that tend to promote and increase intra- project, inter-project and intra-organizational knowledge transfer and learning. Specifically, the researcher notes the distinction between mechanisms used for tacit and explicit knowledge transfer; both tending to promote learning and knowledge transfer through the development of new shared practices. The research shows that the adoption of the mechanisms and processes does not guarantee success unless it is supported by the company environment. Companies should have suitable infrastructure and support processes, to successfully adopt knowledge transfer and learning.

Case Company X is one of the top ten companies in UK, and is a leader in the industry in terms of technological and business development; it also sells a range of products and consultancy services.   They have extensive expertise in project and programme management. In order to maintain their position, they need to have an effective and efficient use of resources. Within this context, the importance of learning and knowledge transfer is important for maintaining a competitive advantage, and improving their performance in project management. They believe that successful implementation of project management does not guarantee that your project will be successful. Instead, it guarantees that the project will be managed effectively, thus improving chances for success. The research conducted shows that Case Company X has institutionalized the procedures and routines to effectively take advantage of the knowledge within the company. Also, measures are undertaken so that learning is facilitated, and it is given top management's attention. Nevertheless, even though there are mechanisms and processes institutionalized, this suggests a feeling of not learning from the lessons learned and mistakes made in the past, and the sharing of knowledge in the current and future projects. Measures need to be taken so that full advantage is taken of the processes and mechanisms that are institutionalized within Case Company X. People within Case Company X need to be more willing to share their knowledge and also utilize to a fuller extent the benefits of the mechanisms and processes which are already put in place.

The researcher's goal was to identify if and to what extent these categories are present at Case Company X, as well as the influence and contribution of these categories to knowledge transfer and learning in and between projects. In this chapter, the recommendations for the problems and issues Case Company X faces will be dealt with. These recommendations will hopefully solve the problems/issues that Case Company X is facing for knowledge transfer and learning. Moreover, hopefully the facilitation of knowledge transfer and learning will be more effective in and between projects. This chapter will answer the research question and provide a list of recommendations for Case Company X.

6.1 Managerial Implications

These findings have implications for practice. The focus on the practice-based nature of knowledge transfer and learning helps to explain the limitations of some existing approaches to capture knowledge and learning from projects. These approaches tend to treat knowledge as independent from its embeddedness within practice, when the practical part is necessary. The researcher's focus on the processes and mechanisms and the difficulties faced suggest that the knowledge transfer and learning in and between projects is even more demanding than it is suggested in practice. It does, however, suggest that the mechanism and processes need to be accompanied by a no-blame and encouraging company environment. Important ingredients in Case Company X were the change in organizational boundaries through creation of new knowledge transfer and learning mechanisms and processes. These applications provided an important incentive for increasing knowledge transfer and improving learning through new shared practices.

The study suggests that top management needs to understand basic assumptions related to knowledge transfer and learning. Top management needs to select those knowledge transfer and learning mechanisms and processes which do not conflict the assumptions in the company. If the chosen mechanisms and processes do not promote sufficient knowledge transfer and learning, they need to be changed. According to Schein (1992), it is challenging and difficult to change basic assumptions, because they are developed over time and exist in people's mind subconsciously. An assumption can be changed only if it is proven to bring positive results. For example, if project managers realize that analyzing lessons learned reports is crucial, they will refer to them in their future projects to a greater extent. Moreover, the mechanisms and processes need to be selected and customized to the specific company context.

Furthermore, as demonstrated in the case study, the implementation of appropriate initiatives (i.e. mechanisms and processes) for knowledge transfer and learning is essential in developing the effective strategies to promote knowledge transfer and learning in and between projects. These initiatives offer a practical avenue for project practitioners to 'practice' knowledge transfer and learning in and between projects, while simultaneously developing and adding-in to their skills.

The researcher suggests that projects create an important arena for generation of knowledge and learning; however, the effectiveness and efficiency of applying such knowledge and learning is shaped by the on-going learning activities of the wider company and its environment.

6.2 Theoretical Implications

These findings make a contribution to project management theory development concerning knowledge transfer and learning in and between projects, and provide researchers new points to further investigate how to increase knowledge transfer and promote learning in and between projects.

The learning landscape which is presented in the analysis chapter represents an empirical example of the set of mechanisms and processes employed by Case Company X to manage knowledge transfer and learning in and between projects. These findings can also be reflected or have direct application in other project settings.

6.3   Recommendations

The researcher will present recommendations for management and project management that could contribute to knowledge transfer and learning in and between projects within Case Company X.

From the analysis chapter it is obvious that Case Company X has implemented many mechanisms and processes which are recommended by the literature reviewed. Nevertheless, the possibility for improvement is given for Company X management.

The following recommendations are proposed to Company X's management:

Emphasize and promote more the importance of learning and knowledge transfer: - awareness of the benefits for knowledge transfer and learning needs to increase. Knowledge management needs to be incorporated in their agenda and be part of the project management plan. Resources need to be invested specifically for knowledge transfer and learning.

Provide a monetary scheme incentive for knowledge transfer - not give incentive only based on performance and milestone achievement, but also on the knowledge transfer and learning promoted. The incentive scheme can be intrinsic or extrinsic, in monetary and non-monetary terms.

Include knowledge transfer and learning in the performance appraisal system - section can be added specifically addressing knowledge transfer and learning. Project managers need to be assessed in relation to the extent of knowledge re-used from previous projects as well as knowledge make available to other projects.

Implement a leaner project organization structure - change the project structure towards a leaner structure, with more project managers involved in the same project. The project management capability will increase, and the knowledge base will be expanded. Nevertheless, the implications of being a partly public governmental company make it challenging to implement a leaner structure.

Make lessons learned compulsory for all projects - lessons learned need to be communicated clearly within the company. The lessons learned database and its benefits should be promoted to a greater extent to all the projects, through formal and informal channels.

Revision and referencing of lessons learned needs to be made compulsory for all the projects currently running and the future projects.

Database and web-portal improvement - provide in depth training in order to utilize to full extent the benefits of the database. The documentation of the projects should be more easily retrievable. The reports, considering their heaviness in quantity, need to be re-structured in mini-reports, wherein specific information required can be allocated with ease. Extending the functions of intranet can facilitate a better flow of information and knowledge sharing.

Time allocated specifically for knowledge transfer and learning - enable qualified personnel to devote their time towards producing a quality lessons learned report. This could be facilitated by assigning junior staff to senior positions, always accompanied by heavy mentoring.

Improve phase review process - tailor the questions of phase review process so that they become more applicable to the project(s) being reviewed.

Streamline all the processes - make the processes more user-friendly. Shorten the time used to fill the paperwork. This would encourage project personnel to challenge the processes more, and be more willing to actually invest their time towards a change for a better future. Streamline the processes so that they can be applicable to all size projects.

Introduce flexibility to the processes - standardization is believed to reduce effectiveness. Flexibility needs to be introduced to the processes, in order to reduce risk and increase effectiveness. Processes are proven frameworks. However, they do not make up for performance. And, they do not substitute creativity. Every project is considered unique and involves uncertainty and risk.

Instill a no-blame culture- encourage personnel to admit their mistakes, and learn from them. Ability to learn from others experiences even if not positive needs to be acknowledged. Therefore, a second chance needs to be given to hard working personnel.

Understand people factor in knowledge transfer and learning – projects are about people, whereas mechanisms and processes tend to focus on management activity mechanism. Balance needs to be established between people and the mechanism, considering the emphasis that is given to skills required to manage knowledge transfer and learning that any project will bring about. Encourage people to commit in the improvement efforts.

6.4   Strengths and Weaknesses

The study has a scientific credibility by using a scientifically accepted method. The literature review provides a grounded theoretical base. The empirical findings are clear and fit with the existing theory. The company which is studied is a respectable and credible company, and the researcher believes that the findings can be applied to other companies of a similar size, operating in a similar industry. The access to best informants for the interviews has been granted, considering that the company initiated the research idea. The interviewees' seniority in the company and years of experience are considered important towards considering the interviewees the best informants.

One weakness can be the fact that access to the documentation and the database has been limited. It is relevant to state that some of the data collected in the interview was sensitive; therefore the research could not use some of the material due to a previously signed non-disclosure agreement. The fact that only one company has been analyzed makes the results not applicable to a more general community. Considering the extensive topic researched, there are many articles and publications in this context, and it can be argued that a considerable number of articles has not been used and referenced for the literature review which provides the theoretical base.

6.5   Recommendations for future research

To increase the credibility and confirm the results of this study, a quantitative research would be the next step. With the usage of statistics in the findings concept, there might be correlations and links discovered in the findings, which were not identified and considered by the researcher of this study. A quantitative study would be more general considering the higher number of respondents and companies involved. Moreover, the quantitative study would enable a further generalization of the results across industries and other similar companies. In addition, if it is put in a cost perspective, the knowledge learning and transfer could be understood in terms of the economic gain of its implementation.

Also, determining the right amount of knowledge transfer could be proposed as a question for future research. This would imply to settle of what is the optimal level of knowledge transfer and learning.

6.6   Final comments

The main contribution of this study lies in the investigation of the current mechanisms and processes institutionalized that foster knowledge transfer and learning within Case Company X. Moreover, the identification of the environment of the company has been made, in order to understand if it promotes or hinders knowledge transfer and learning.

The researcher hopes that this study will increase and contribute to the awareness of Case Company X, towards the benefits of facilitating knowledge transfer and learning. This awareness could be used to gain a competitive advantage and sustain and improve their position in the industry and worldwide.

Case Company X has a myriad of projects, at different stages of completion, as well as projects planned to start in the near future. The challenge lies in understanding which of the mechanisms and processes have the highest potential for creating knowledge, transferring knowledge and promoting learning.

Knowledge transfer and learning will be important for the future of the companies. The mechanisms and processes are continuously evolving and maturing. This is demonstrated by the increased number of researches done in this field.

REFERENCES

A Guide to Project Management Body of Knowledge (PMBOK) (2004). third edn, Pennsylvania, USA, Project Management Institute Inc.

Argyris, C. (1999). *On organizational learning,* second edn. Oxford, Blackwell.

Association of Project Management (APM) (2004). *Project Risk Analysis and Management Guide,* High Wycombe, Buckinghamshire, UK, APM Publishing Limited, pp.104-105.

Association of Project Management (APM) (2006). *APM Body of Knowledge,* fifth edn, High Wycombe, Buckinghamshire, UK, APM Publishing Limited.

Association of Project Management (APM) (2008). *APM Competence Framework,* High Wycombe, Buckinghamshire, UK, APM Publishing Limited.

Association of Project Management (APM) (2008). *Introduction to Project Planning,* High Wycombe, Buckinghamshire, UK, APM Publishing Limited.

Association of Project Management (APM) (2008). Complex Programmes, A 'whole systems' approach, *Project - The Voice of Project Management,* 21(1), High Wycombe, Buckinghamshire, UK, APM Publishing Limited, pp.18-20.

Ayas, K. (1996). Professional project management: a shift towards learning and a knowledge creating structure, *International Journal of Project Management,* 14 (3), pp. 131-136.

Ayas, K. (1997). Integrating corporate learning with project management, *International Journal of Production Economics,* 51 (1-2), pp.61-76.

Ayas, K. & Zenuik, N. (2001). Project-based learning: building communities of reflective practitioners, *Management Learning,* 31(1), 61-67.

Baumard, P. (1999). *Tacit Knowledge in Organization,* SAGE Publications Ltd, London, UK.

Bayer, F., Enparantza, R., Maier, R., Obermair, F. & Schmiedinger, B., Know-CoM: Decentralized Knowledge Management Systems for Cooperating Die- and- Mold- Making

SMEs: In Jennex, M. (2005) (Editor) , *Case Studies in Knowledge Management*, pp. 186 - 208 .

Becerra-Fernandez, I., Gonzales, A. & Sabherwal, R. (2004). *Knowledge Management and KM Software Package.* First end, USA, Prentice Hall, Pearson Education.

Blumberg, B., Cooper, D. & Schindler, P. (2005). *Business Research Methods.* UK: McGraw Hill Education.

Bollinger, A.S. & Smith, R.D. 2001. Managing organizational knowledge as a strategic asset, *Journal of Knowledge Management,* 5 (1), pp. 8-18.

Brady, T., Marshall, N., Prencipe, A. & Tell, F. (2003). Making sense of learning landscapes in project-based organizations, *presented at the 3rd European Conference on Organizing, Knowledge and Capabilities*, Athens, Greece.

Brady, T. & Davies, A. (2004). Building project capabilities: From exploratory to exploitative learning, *Organizational Studies,* 25(9), pp. 1601-1621.

Brown, S. & Eisenhardt, K. (1996). Leveraging product innovation: innocent traps, adaptive organizations and strategic evolution, *Paper presented at the Academy of Management's 56th Annual Meeting, Cincinnati.*

Bryman, A. & Bell, E. (2003). *Business Research Methods,* New York: Oxford University Press Inc.

Busby, J. (1999). An assessment of post-project reviews, *Project Management Journal,* 30(3), pp.23-29.

Byrne, M. (2001). Understanding Life Experiences through a Phenomenological Approach to Research. Retrieved 23 November 2008 from
http://findarticles.com/p/articles/mi_m0FSL/is_4_73/ai_73308177/pg_4

Carillo, P., Robinson, H., Al-Ghassani, A. & Anumba, C. (2004). Knowledge management in UK construction: Strategies, resources and barriers, *International Journal of Project Management,* 35 (1), pp. 46-56.

Coakes, E., Bradburn, A. & Blake, K., Knowledge Management in a Project Climate: In Jennex, M. (2005) (Editor), *Case Studies in Knowledge Management, pp.* 130-138.

Cooper, K.G., Lynesis, J.M. & Bryant, B.J. (2002). Learning to learn, from past to future, *International Journal of Project Management,* 20 (3), pp.213-219.

Cowan, R. & Foray, D. (1997). The economics of codification and the diffusion of knowledge, *Industrial and Corporate Change,* 6(3), 595-622.

Davenport, T.H., Eccles, R.G. & Prusak, L. (1992). Information politics, *Sloan Management Review,* 34 (1), pp. 53-64.

Davenport, T.H. & Prusak, L. (1998). *Working Knowledge: How Organizations Manage What They Know,* Harvard Business School Press.

Davies, A. & Hobday, M. (2005). The *Business of Projects: Managing Innovation in Complex Products and Systems,* Cambridge University Press.

DeFillippi, R. J. (2001). Introduction: project-based learning, reflective practices and learning outcomes, *Management Learning,* 32(1), 5-10.

DeFillippi, R.J. & Arthur, M.B. (1998). Paradox in project-base enterprise: the case of film making, *California Management Review,* 40(2), 125-139.

Disteter, G. (2002). Management of project knowledge and experiences, *Journal of Knowledge Management,* 6(5), pp. 512-520.

Dixon, N.M. (2000). *Common Knowledge: How Companies Thrive by Sharing What They Know',* Boston: Harvard Business School Press.

Drucker, P.F. (1993). *Post Capitalist Society,* Harper Business, New York.

Gardiner, P. D. (2005). *Project Management: A strategic planning approach,* Palgrave MacMillan: Hampshire, UK.

Gilbert, M. & Cordey- Hayes, M. (1996). Understanding the process of knowledge transfer to achieve successful technological innovation, *Technovation,* 16(6), pp. 301-312.

Ginev, D. (1995). Between epistemology and hermeneutics, *Science & Education*, 4(2), pp.147-159.

Glaser, B. G. & Strauss, A. L. (1967). *The discovery of grounded theory: strategies for qualitative research*, Chicago: Aldine.

Grant, K.P. (2006). Leveraging project team expertise for better project solutions, Paper presented at the *PMI Research Conference 2006*, Montréal.

Guba, E.G., & Lincoln, Y.S. (1994). *Competing paradigms in qualitative research*, In Denzin & Lincoln (1994). pp. 105-117.

Gulliver, F.R. (1987). Post-project appraisals pay, *Harvard Business Review,* 65(2), pp.128-132.

Hahn, T., Schmiedinger B. & Stephan, E., Supporting Research and Development Process Using Knowledge Management Methods: In Jennex, M. (2005) (Editor), Case *Studies in Knowledge Management, pp.165*-186.

Hamel, G. (2002). *Leading the Revolution*, Plume, New York.

Hameri, A.P. & Nihtilä, J. (1998). Data-based learning in product development, *Scandinavian Journal of Management,* 14(3), pp.223-238.

Harvey, M., Palmer, J., & Speier, C. (1998). Implementing intraorganizational learning: A phased-model approach supported by intranet technology, *European Management Journal,* 16(3), pp.341-354.

Hatami, A. & Galliers, R.D., Exploring the Impact of Knowledge (Re)use and Organizational Memory on the Effectiveness of Strategic Decisions: A Longitudinal Case Study, : In Jennex, M. (2005) (Editor) ,*Case Studies in Knowledge Management ,*pp. 66- 80.

Hauschild, S., Licht, T. & Stein, W. (2001). Creating a knowledge culture, *The McKinsey Quarterly*, Vol.2001 (1), pp. 74-81.

Hobday, M. (2000). The project based organization: An ideal form for managing complex products and systems? , *Research Policy,* 29 (7-8), pp.871-893.

Jennex, M. (2005). *Case studies in Knowledge Management*, Idea Group Publishing, London, UK.

Karlsen, J.T. & Gottschalk, P. (2004). Factors affecting knowledge transfer in IT projects, *Engineering Management Journal*, 16 (1).

Keegan, A. & Turner, R.J. (2001). Quantity versus quality in project-based learning practices, *Management Learning*, 31(1), 77-98.

Koskinen, K.U. (2004). Knowledge management to improve project communication and implementation, *International Journal of Project Management*, 35(2), 13-19.

Koskinen, K.U., Pihlanto, P., & Vanharanta, H. (2003). Tacit Knowledge Sharing in a Project Work Context, *International Journal of Project Management*, 21(4), 281-190.

Kotnour, T. (1999). A learning framework for project management, *Project Management Journal*, 30 (2), pp. 32-38.

Kotnour, T. (2000). Organizational learning practices in the project management environment, *International Journal of Quality & Reliability Management*, 17 (4/5), pp. 393-406.

Lambe, P. (2004). Practical Techniques for Complex Knowledge Transfer. Retrieved 3 November 2008 from www.greencameleon.com

Lampel, J., Scarbrough, H. & Macmillan, S. (2008). Managing through projects in knowledge based environment, *Long Range Planning*, 41 (1), pp. 7-16.

Lawrence, P.R. & Lorsch, J.W. (1967). *Organization and environment: Managing diffentiation and integration*, Harvard University Press.

Leseure, M.J. & Brookes, N.J. (2004). Knowledge management benchmarks for project management, *Journal of Knowledge Management*, 8(1), pp.103-116.

Li, Z., Yezhuang, T. & Pong. L., Organizational Knowledge Sharing Based on the ERP Implementation of Yongxin Paper Co., Ltd: In Jennex, M. (2005) (Editor), Case *Studies in Knowledge Management*, pp. 155- 163.

Liikamma, K. (2006). Tacit Knowledge and competencies of project manager, *Tampere University of Technology, Publication 628,* Tampere.

Lindkvist, L., Soderlund, J. & Tell, F. (1998). Managing product development projects: On the significance of fountains and deadlines, *Organization Studies,* 19 (6), pp. 931-951.

Martensson, M. (2000). A critical review of knowledge management as a management tool, *Journal of Knowledge Management,* 4 (3), pp. 204-216.

Miles, M.B. & Huberman, A.M. (1994). *An Expanded Sourcebook: Qualitative Data Analysis,* second edn, UK: Sage Publications.

Mooradian, N. (2005). Tacit knowledge: Philosophic roots and role in KM, *Journal of Knowledge Management,* 9(6), pp.104-113.

Müller, R. (2009). *Project Governance,* Gower Publishing, Aldeshot, UK.

Mumford, A. (1994). Four approaches to learning from experience, *The Learning Organization,* 1(1), pp.4-10.

Nahapiet, J., & Ghosal, S. (1998). Social capital, intellectual capital, and the organizational advantage, *The Academy of Management Review,* 23(2), 242-266.

Nonaka, I. (1991). The Knowledge-Creating Company, *Harvard Business Review,* 69 (6), p. 96.

Nonaka, I. & Takeuchi, H. (1995). *The Knowledge-Creating Company: How Japanese Companies Create the Dynamics of Innovation,* Oxford University Press New York.

Owen, J. & Burstein, F. Where Knowledge Management Resides Within Project Management,: In Jennex, M. (2005) (Editor) , *Case Studies in Knowledge Management,* pp. 138-153.

Pemberton, J. & Stonehouse, & G.H. (2000). Organizational learning and knowledge assets - an essential partnership, *The Learning Organization: An International Journal,* 7 (4), pp. 184 - 194.

Polanyi, M. (1967*). The Tacit Dimension, London,* Routledge & Kegan, Paul.

Prencipe, A. & Tell, F. (2001). Inter-project learning: processes and outcomes of knowledge codification in project-based firms, *Research Policy,* 30(9), pp.1373-1394.

Reich, B.H. (2007). Managing knowledge and learning in IT projects: A conceptual framework and guidelines for practice, *International Journal of Project Management,* 38(2), pp. 5-17.

Reich, B.H. & Wee, S.Y. (2006). Searching for knowledge in the PMBOK guide, *International Journal of Project Management,* 37(2), pp.11-26.

Remenyi, D., Williams, B., Money, A. & Swartz, E. (1998). *Doing Research in Business and Management, An Introduction to Process and Methods.* London, UK: Sage Publication.

Roth, G & Kleiner, A. (1998). Developing organizational memory through learning histories, *Organizational Dynamics,* 27(2), pp. 43-60.

Saunders, M., Lewis, P. & Thornhill, A. (2003). *Research Methods for Business Students.* England: Pearson Education Limited.

Schein, E.H. (1992). *Organizational Culture and Leadership,* second edn, San Francisco: Jossey Bass.

Schindler, M. & Eppler, M.J. (2003). Harvesting project knowledge: a review of project learning methods and success factors, *International Journal of Project Management,* 21(3), pp. 219-228.

Sense, A.J. (2007). Structuring the project environment for learning, *International Journal of Project Management,* 25 (4), pp. 405-412.

Sense, A.J. (2008). The conditioning of project participants' authority to learn within projects, *International Journal of Project Management,* 26 (2), pp. 105-111.

Skyrme, D.J. (1998). Developing a Knowledge Strategy. Retrieved 2 November 2008 from http://www.skyrme.com/pubs/knwstrat.htm

Söderlund, J., Vaagaasar, A.L., & Andersen, E.S. (2008). Relating, reflecting and routinizing: Developing project competence in cooperation with others, *International Journal of Project Management,* 26 (5), pp. 517-526.

Spender, J.C. (1996). Making knowledge the basis of a dynamic theory of the firm, *Strategic Management Journal*, 17, Winter Special Issue, pp. 45-62.

Thiry, M. & Deguire, J. (2007). Recent developments in project-based organizations, *International Journal of Project Management,* 25(7), pp. 649-658.

Trochim, W.M. (2006). Positivism and Post-Positivism, Research Method Knowledge Base. Retrieved 19 November 2008 from http://socialresearchmethods.net/kb/positvsm.php

Turner, R.J. & Müller, R. (2003). On the nature of the project as a temporary organization, *Internal Journal of Project Management,* 21(1), pp.1-8.

Wenger, E. (1998). *Communities of practice: learning, meaning and identity,* Cambridge: Cambridge University Press.

Wilke, H. (1998). *Systemisches Wissensmanagement,* Lucius and Lucius Werlagsgesellschaft.

Williams, T. (2003). Learning from projects, *Journal of the Operational Research Society,* 54 (5), pp. 443-451.

Williams, T. (2004). Identifying the hard lessons from projects-easily, *International Journal of Project Management,* 22 (4), pp. 273-279.

Woo J.H., Clayton, M.J., Johnson, R.E., Flores, B.E., & Ellis, C. (2004). Dynamic knowledge map: reusing experts' tacit knowledge in the AEC industry, Automation *in Construction,* 13, pp.203-207.

Zack, M.H. (1999). Managing codified knowledge, *Sloan Management Review,* 40(4), pp.45-58.

Zollo, M. & Winter, G. (2001). Knowledge and the speed of the transfer and imitation of organizational capabilities: An empirical test, *Organization Science,* 6(1), 76.92.

INTERVIEWS

Interview 1. PMO Manager – Programme 1

Personal background

The person has an engineering background, and has been in Case Company X since 1994. He initially started working in the Engineering Center, continued with Product Control Office, became head of Installation Resources, then senior project planner before becoming the PMO manager which position he currently holds.

The PMO office is under the Programme 1, which is one of the main six programmes Case Company X runs. There are a total of 20 ongoing projects running. The PMO manager talks about the Project Management Plan (PMP) which is compulsory to be drafted by all the projects. The PMP incorporates the tasks list, the beginning and the ending date of the project as well as the resources allocated for the work packages. It is divided into the fixed and the variable PMP. The PMO Manager explains that the fixed PMP contains the *"objectives, scope, and how the project is going to be managed".* Compulsory to this, the variable PMP is developed, containing *"up to date reporting, which helps the PMO office to track and monitor progress of the project in terms of – cost, risk and schedule".* He describes the project model consist of three main phases: Feasibility and Options, Product Development and Implementation. The PMO Manager states that all the projects follow the similar structure; nevertheless, there are additional phases which can be added, depending on the specifics of the project.

The project managers and the team members are assigned based on their skills and abilities. He states that even though Case Company X is a technically oriented company, technical skills are not mandatory for all the project members and managers. He says that as long as the *"person comprehends the scope and delivers the project"* it is enough to prove that you are right for the job. *"Patience, diplomatic skills, and commitment are the most important traits for a PM"* he says, adding also that *"you need to believe in the project".* He states that there are the same people involved in different projects, which makes their job *"more interesting and refreshing if involved in more than one project".* He states that the fact that the same people are used in different projects contributes to the learning process and knowledge sharing.

During the projects there are different feedback routines. The PMO manager states that to ensure that everything is in accordance with the policies and regulations, there are quality assurance audits conducted for their projects. There are three types of reviews/audits: internal, independent and external reviews/audits. Internal reviews/audits are done continuously (i.e. phase reviews and project reviews); independent audits are done once a month or three months (i.e. monthly reviews and CPR), whereas external audits are done by a third party (i.e. external party to company). The third party decides on the combination of projects to be audited without prior notice to Case Company X.

Project review meetings are conducted wherein important topics are discussed, with a prior developed agenda, and reporting done by different PM(s) and project team members. Furthermore, issues and actions are captured, and a *"target date set to clear actions"* is set during meetings. Their frequency of meetings is specific to the nature and urgency of the project; nevertheless, there is a compulsory requirement for meetings to be held at least once a month. All the project team members are present in the project review meetings, so that everyone is informed and up-to-date with the recent events and decisions made. In addition, there are external reviews/audits conducted, which he feels contributes to the successfulness of the project and to the outcomes being *"more credible and independent"*. The projects are subject to Critical Project Reviews (CPR), done internally within Case Company X, but independent of the project members and PM. He emphasizes that all projects are subject to reviews, and he feels that reviews are especially important in long duration projects, because he fears that too much time can go by, important facts will be forgotten and they will be unable to be tracked down. At Case Company X, the project duration ranges from six months to three years and the number of people within a project range from 4 to 50.

Within their projects there is a minimum requirement to produce lessons learned at the end of the project, nevertheless, they encourage lessons learned to be produced also during the phase reviews of the project. The lessons learned are recorded in written format, and he explains that Case Company X has specific templates designed to be filled, which are uploaded automatically in the Company's central repository –database-. He especially emphasizes that when a new project is launched, a requirement is to use the lessons learned from previous projects. Nevertheless he says that *"the ratio of people using lessons learned when a new project comes on board is 80-20 %"*. According to him, the reasons why some people do not use the lessons learned is because *"it is difficult to hunt around what is specifically required for your project"*.

They have a central repository system- a database -which is a search engine, enabling PM(s) under each project to submit technical reports and store them under the project's *"Master Record Index (MRI)"*. There are specific templates within the database to store information, which makes it easier for the PM(s) and team members because there is no need to upload documents, considering that the templates can be updated and saved directly. Special emphasis is given to the changes and *"what went wrong and what went right during the project"*. But, he states that the *"the central repository- database- where the lessons learned are stored was not a user-friendly database, but with many complaints of people who had to deal with it and use it, it got improved in the past six months"*. The access of the project team in the database is limited, as he says that *"only those who need to have access to the database- have access to it "*.

Regarding processes used by projects in this particular program, he explains that the process descriptions are generally the same for all projects. They are part of the governance set and descriptions called *"Case Company X Management Standard Value"*. The description of processes is done in Flowchart from Micrografix (Circles, arrows and squares). The process description is presented orally to all the team members, and it is done in the way which enables the team members to see the whole picture and not only their specific task. He says that the processes are functioning well within the Company, but of course his attitude is that *"there is always room for improvement"*. According to PMO Manager, processes are well embraced among the personnel using them, they are user friendly to a certain extent, and most people like to use them. On the other hand, there is a small percentage of people that doesn't like to use them, but according to him, they start using the processes because they *"realize the massive value of using the processes in getting the job done"*. If there is a major new process planned to be launched, Case Company X organizes introduction sessions wherein all the PM(s) are invited to participate. Then, PM(s) disseminate their knowledge on the process to their team members.

There are routines to store people's experiences and knowledge that are not written down, with the goal of preventing loss of knowledge if people change jobs. Even though, according to PMO Manager *"the good thing about Case Company X is that people don't leave"*. During the projects, there are *"succession sessions"* conducted once a year within Case Company X. He explains that the goal of the succession sessions is to *"identify who could replace the person – or succeed the person- if he/she decides to leave the company"*. In this way, Case Company X is prepared also in case people decide to leave the company unexpectedly.

PMO Managers' stand is that Case Company X knowledge is diffused properly across all projects through formal ways mostly, as mentioned above. But also, there are informal channels which are considered important for the company. For example, if he is facing a problem with a project, he can *"walk across the other programme or projects and ask how to solve it"*. He has also participated in retreats that are organized three times a year, with an overnight duration, outside company premises. Herein, the informal discussions and sharing of experience is done in relation to work and current ongoing projects within the programme. This facilitates the tacit knowledge sharing among the PM(s) which contributes to the learning in the long term. Another example he elaborates upon is the gatherings that are organized by Case Company X, inviting all the PM(s) for a discussion with the Senior Programme Manager, within company premises. The benefit of these gatherings is that PM(s) discuss the problems and express any concerns and dissatisfactions they have during their work.

The PMO manager recognizes the way of thinking in the company that you should always try to share your knowledge and experience. As per people who feel that they need to keep their knowledge to themselves, he says that it doesn't help and *"you need to be giving in order to receive"*. The management of the company emphasizes the importance of the company being a knowledge-based company, wherein the employees are considered to be the most important resource. He says that people within the company are aware of the overall vision of the company, and they work for the benefit of the company. He states that management contributes resources to facilitate learning and knowledge management.

Also, there are workshops organized, usually during lunch time, in order to share knowledge and present *"burning topics which are to be discussed and exposed"*. The invitations to the workshop are sent throughout Case Company X, and it is of interest to people because the workshops discuss and present *"certain topics that people want information on"*.

PMO Manager feels that the feedback routines, the processes and its knowledge creating culture enabled Case Company X to become *"world leader in project management delivery"* and *"Case Company X is in a good place in terms of project management capability"*.

He thinks that an additional procedure which could be applied by Case Company X is that in the final project closure meetings, it would be good practice to invite PM(s) that didn't work in the specific project being closed. This would create a productive discussion environment. He feels that with this *"PM(s) will gain first hand information on the bads'and goods' of the project, and knowledge will be shared among different projects"*.

The person has an Electronic Engineering background, and has been in Case Company X since 1997. He initially started working in the Engineering Center as a System Engineer for four years, he continued in a Business Analyst position for three years, and then became a Project Manager which position he currently holds.

The project he leads has the goal of establishing a Contingency facility, in order to relocate the employees. The project has officially started a year ago, but he personally joined the project six months ago, emphasizing that the project was *"at a difficult place"* when he started. He specifies that *"Contingency Center"* project is a part of a larger programme within Case Company X. The project is expected to last for another year. The total number of staff in this project is 50, wherein he says that most of the team members tend to be selected from the criteria on who is the best available technical/engineering person, because of the engineering nature of the project. Nevertheless, he feels that in many cases other qualities can be beneficial for achieving results in the project. He illustrates with the fact that *"general managers of air traffic control centers can be of engineering background, and with no knowledge on air trafficking control, but still be the managers of air traffic controllers"*. For him it is important for PM to have the ability to allocate the resources within the company, and deliver the requested output. Also, the presences of *"soft skills, especially communication"* are important for his team members, especially when it has to do with personal interfaces with the customers.

Project staffing is extracted from the *"work centers"*, which represent the pool of resources, and they are temporarily assigned to the project. He feels that it would be ideal if there is a consistent crew of team members, because they would dedicate themselves fully to the project. Moreover, people that are experts are known to the PM(s), and everyone tries to get them on board. This raises a conflict of HR resources; nevertheless, the final saying is made based on which project is considered of more priority for Case Company X. Nevertheless, he feels that since the same people are working in different projects, it contributes to significant knowledge transfer between projects. The fact that the same people are involved in the future projects enables learning by drawing knowledge from their previous experiences. *"Project is used as a vehicle to transfer knowledge"* he states. He believes that the challenge lies in representing technical realities in artifacts that cloak the engineering complexity.

He gives special importance to building relationships and getting along with people in his project team as well as with the stakeholders of the project. It is important to establish a relationship because *"it helps when there is a need to have the difficult conversation if needed under specific circumstances"*. He describes his style of managing people based on respect and mutual understanding, by also making it clear that project team members have *"management accountability, on top of the explicitly stated deliveries in their work packages which need to be fulfilled"*.

He stated that the project reviews are held once a month during the project duration, and they are aimed at reviewing costs and schedules but also lessons learned. The outcome of lessons learned and closeout projects are incorporated in the specific template produced by Case Company X. Interviewee argued that the written documents also capture the process that underlies the lessons learned or closeout projects procedure. PM stated that he practices lessons learned meetings on a continuous basis, not only at the end-of-phase of his project. These meetings have a pre-set agenda, which incorporates progress updates, the next week plans of the key team members present in the meetings, financial issues – cost optimization, risks arising and any other emergent issue arising that has not been predicted beforehand. The output of these meetings is recorded in the actions log, which is part of the variable PMP, and a direct link to it is provided in the database. Moreover, the benefit with actions log is that it can be typed directly and recorded in the database, and a target date is set to undertake the action.

In addition, he has adopted the lifecycle approach which is specified also in the company's process for lessons learned. There is end-of-phase lessons learned sessions conducted, wherein key team members participate, and lessons learned report is produced at the end of the month. The report is stored in the project's MRI. He explains that in consensus with his team members, they decide on the 5 key learning points and highlight them in the lessons learned report. Whereas in most of the cases the end-of-phase meetings are held by PM(s), he prefers to have an external independent facilitator for the meeting, to ensure credibility. The outcomes of the end-of-phase meetings are used to produce the lessons learned report, which can be allocated under his project MRI in the database.

Even though he faces a meeting overload, the interviewee values lessons learned meetings and reports because they offer the environment to reflect on past actions and identify what could be used and carried not only to the next phase of the project, but also to other projects in the future. In addition, he feels that lessons learned meetings and reports enable him and his team members to reflect upon their actions, by trying to understand and improve them, and also articulate them in written form. Considering that he has joined the project six months after it started, he personally has used the lessons learned from previous projects as an aid to help him give direction to his project, considering that when he joined the *"project was at a bad place"*. He has accessed the lessons learned from the database, which he thinks is not a very user friendly tool, and he considers that *"it is a grown-up tool the full potential of which is not explored by employees of Case Company X"*. The training received in usage of the database is provided by the company, but not in much depth.

He believes that most people are not particularly keen on using the processes. *"If you ask a person to go from A to B, he would rather have an option of choosing the way to reach there rather than being imposed a process to follow"*, he says. Nevertheless, he feels that most of the processes used by Case Company X are *"more or less"* user-friendly, and that *"they are there for a reason"*. Processes are put in place to ensure Case Company X that the projects deliver the outputs all the way through and not only at the end of the project. Moreover, the processes give confidence to Case Company X that the projects are running according to the plan set up beforehand. Nevertheless, his attitude is that *"there is always room for improvement in processes"* and Case Company X is working on *"changes to streamline and improve them"*.

Even though there is a mainly procedure-oriented culture, it does not reduce the importance of people-to-people communication and informal knowledge transfer. According to PM, the project learning occurs through people and informal channels. He personally practices to have meetings with the PM(s) on an informal basis or as he calls them *"informal chats"*, which he did with the PM who had a similar project running within Case Company X. He believes that these informal chats contribute to overall knowledge sharing because he can ensure in this way that the mistakes that happened in the previous project are not repeated in his project, and also it gives him and his team a *"head start on the project"*. Another example of informal, people-based approach to inter-project learning that he practices is his one-to-one meeting with the people in charge of the work packages in his project. He has *"10-15 such individual meetings per week"* because he wants to be updated on the latest events within his projects, and to ensure that the project team members are satisfied and understand their role in the project.

The company has developed a Programme Development and Finance Organization (PDFO) as a knowledge sharing initiative. The aim of this entity created is to develop, implement, and maintain formal procedures (most of the time ICT –based) for project managers. According to the interviewee, the company is well experienced in a procedure oriented culture. He specifically states the importance of the governance system which runs within Case Company X, and the senior management buy-in of the processes and mechanisms used. He feels that *"if there was no support of management of Case Company X, none of the processes would enable us to achieve the desired results"*.

Nevertheless, he is not particularly keen on *"phase review process"*, and he hopes that in the future *"the questions which are in the phase review will be more relevant to actual project being reviewed"*. Furthermore he states the need to have more detailed guidelines in answering the posed questions, otherwise the risk of misunderstanding and wrong answers being provided is high.

Interview 3. Senior Programme Manager – Programme 2

Personal background

The person has an engineering background. He had the position of X programme manager before becoming the Senior Programme Manager which position he currently holds.

The Senior Programme Manager (SPM) described the importance of the Programme 2 p for Case Company X. The SPM talks therefore most of the programme 2, which nature is different and unique as compared to other projects which were conducted in Case Company X. He says that it is *"not a project as such, but it is a project which will be conducted in cooperation with other partners in Europe"*. The definition phase started in 2003, and ended early this year, and the development phase is expected to continue for 8 years. Then, the implementation phase will start to put in place the operational services, which will go on beyond 2020. For the moment, the project doesn't have an official end date, to which SPM adds that *"it is not planned to that level of granularity"*. Also, considering the current workload, there is only a team of 4 people reporting, with another 20 people helping in the bid project.

The reason why there is currently only one project within the programme is because they are currently involved in the bidding phase, which is the consequent phase after the definition phase of the project. He added that the specific nature of the project, and the cooperation with many other entities has created a new project model not following the standard Case Company X phases. Case Company X was involved in the definition phase which was completed earlier this year. They are now biding for the development phase, which incorporates the development of R&D and concepts of operation, prototypes will be built. The bidding phase is *"unusual for Case Company X"* wherein SPM compares it to *"commercial organization bidding for work"*. Moreover, there will be project management processes which will be applied if found appropriate, as well as bid management processes which are different.

Nevertheless, considering the specific and different nature of this project/programme, he strongly believes that it will ensure that the knowledge gained from bidding and executing such a project will become embedded in company's memory and lessons learned produced will be used in future projects of similar nature.

Currently, the project has only the fixed part of the PMP. The variable part will be written once the reporting format and the processes are available to them, nevertheless, it doesn't mean that will look the same as in usual Case Company X projects, but the purpose will be the same and it will cover the same essentials.

Regarding the de-briefing methods utilized in his programme, the weekly meetings are present, wherein *"we are updated on where we are so far"*. Also, sometimes meetings take form of teleconference considering the requirement of movement and establishment of team members on site, but he states that team members are encouraged strongly to be present in the meetings. SPM says that in his project the minutes of meetings are held and they are distributed in form of an email to all the participants. cMoreover, the key decisions are recorded in the issues and actions log, which are stored in the project's MRI, held in control and configured in the database.

When asked on other feedback routines, he replies that there are internal monthly review meetings, with the purpose of reviewing the financial situation of the project, and informing the relevant parties. He specifies that in this particular project considering that it is different and specific being a bidding phase, it is *"difficult to develop timescales because they are out of my hand"*. He says that *"once the project gets to its full extent, it will be subject to formal reviews – i.e. phase reviews and critical project reviews organized within Case Company X"*. Nevertheless, he is very familiar with the critical project reviews in his past projects and programmes, wherein he states that he applies some of the methodologies to his project/programme monthly reviews but at a lighter scale. They also cover processes, issues, costs, opportunities, resources, but not to a deep level of detail because he finds it unnecessary.

He argues that considering that they are not in the project yet, the lessons learned have not been produced yet, considering that they are typically produced at the end- of the phase or end of project. Moreover, after the bidding phase, he gathered the team in order to get feedback on *"what the team thought went bad and what went well"*. The team members were asked to answer some questions in written form before they came to the meeting and the output was recorded. Nevertheless, the respondent states this was a more informal lessons learned produced after the bidding phase, and *"before the non-binding offer"*. This was done with the purpose of making sure that all the relevant information is covered when we produce *"the binding offer"*. On the question of using the lessons learned from previous projects, the respondent replied that they have used the lessons learned developed from Programme definition phase, considering that this project/programme is new to Case Company X and there are no previous lessons learned produced which can be applied specifically to the programme. He finds the lessons learned very useful in order to prevent and control negative events from reoccurring, and he argues that *"lessons learned are picked-up all the time, not only during meetings, but also during your experience"*. He recognizes the benefit of informal ways of knowledge sharing, which he applied by speaking to different people involved in the definition phase and trying to learn from their experiences.

Interestingly, Case Company X does not link the meetings and reviews with its appraisal system. There are no incentive systems in terms of promotion or higher payments linked to the actual knowledge sharing (i.e. implementation of lessons learned meetings and producing reports). SPM says *"the only motivation is in improving the process, so that the overall performance is improved"*. Case Company X rewards project managers in relation to performance indicators of the project (i.e. key performance indicators and milestones) but doesn't evaluate project managers in relation to project learning performance indicators. With other words, the project managers are not assessed in relation to the extent of knowledge re-used from previous projects and/or project knowledge made available to other projects (for instance via meetings, progress reviews, closeout reports).

He thinks that an incentive scheme would be one aspect of behavior as a team. The appraisal process within Case Company X is related to behaviors and team collaboration, and not specific to knowledge sharing. He believes that it is important to establish a joint code of conduct helped with maintaining positive behavior, engendering trust, agreement and mutual benefits. Nevertheless, he thinks that appraisal systems could be changed in the direction of *"encompassing more the sharing of knowledge and lessons learned"*.

On the processes currently used by Case Company X, he feels that *"there is always room for improvement"*. He does not think that processes make cover for performance in organizations. He says that in Case Company X there have been steady improvements in processes over the last 4-5 years. His personal feeling is that now *"processes are too onerous and to expensive"*. A lot of the processes that were adapted by Case Company X are rooted from the experience of the different project members utilizing processes in other organizations. He thinks that some of the processes are user- friendly and some are not. Moreover, he feels that the time used for filling out paperwork for completing the processes could be used for *"more value-adding activities"*. He believes that since the maturity of the

Case Company X as a project organization has increased, it is time decrease the processes and make it more streamlined. Some of the governance processes don't fit the size of the projects, especially considering that Case Company X will deal with a small number of big projects and a big number of relatively small projects in the next 2-3 years. He simply believes that the current processes are *"too heavy"* for the projects that Case Company X will have in the future.

He seems to be satisfied with the level of training his employees receive, and believes that Case Company X does its duty in training people well. In general he thinks that Case Company X is a knowledge based organization, keen to share and transfer knowledge within their premises but as well as with the cooperating entities. The problem is with the people, and their willingness to refer to the lessons learned produced. He feels that once the lessons learned reports are produced and put in the database, no one will go back and look at them.

He believes that the main knowledge lies *"in people's heads"*, and is the most important and the most difficult knowledge to articulate and codify. He feels that people leaving the jobs and then being transferred to other departments contributes to the loss of knowledge and is a considerable problem. On the question of how to deal with this problem, the respondent replied that it would be good during the phase reviews and the kick off meetings to make it compulsory to read the previous lessons learned from projects similar to the current ones, as well as to produce and store the lessons learned from phase reviews. He believes that it needs to be compulsory, in order to *"provide a trigger and promote thought of using the lessons learned to people"*.

He doesn't deny the importance of informal channels of knowledge transfer. *"Case Company X has different informal mechanisms"* he says. One of them is the informal weekly meetings of SPM(s), whereas issues of interest are shared and discussed. Specifically, in his programme there are informal chats with the other entities involved in the programme, which is in a form of a forum. He states that forums represent the informal knowledge sharing. He specified the relationship of Case Company X with (APM), which is of crucial importance. He personally has been part of several workshops organized by APM, and occasionally has been a guest speaker especially on the programme 3 topic.

Considering that this programme is in cooperation with other organizations, he feels there is a general will of the organizations to share knowledge and to work in a collaborative manner. But he specifies that no-one has previously tried to develop a pan-European air traffic management system before, therefore, it is a rather new experience for all the involved entities. It represents a challenge for all involved parties.

There is a need to make sure that the processes are trimmed a bit, to be suitable to the smaller projects which Case Company X will have in the future. Case Company X is a great organization to work for, and he says that *"we are lucky to have slightly more resources which means that people have more time to help other people"*. If compared to previous organizations he has worked in, there was always competition in terms of resources, which he believes contributes negatively to lessons learned because people are too busy and concentrate on the delivery and less or not at all on knowledge sharing and transfer.

Interview 4. Project Quality Manager – Programme 3

The person has a Quality Assurance background, and has been in Case Company X since 2004. He initially started working as a consultant and contractor before being officially hired by Case Company X and becoming a Project Manager which position he currently holds. He worked in the project environment all of his working life.

The project quality manager is the *'supervisor'* of all the quality managers participating in different projects, but as well as he works as a Quality Manager (QM) within projects. The projects he is currently working on are part of programmes. He considers himself well experienced in Long Term Investment Projects within Case Company X. He feels that it is better to work in bigger projects rather than smaller ones, because the amount of resources allocated is bigger (i.e. time and money) which enables him to work into more detail on preventive measures and ensure quality is delivered. The competition for resources in small projects results in *"people spending only that time necessary to get the project happening and minimal time of reflection and deeper learning"* he says. He feels that projects with informally perceived higher profiles gain more attention and participant effort than those considered lower is status, and the former attracts more participant effort on learning activity.

He specifies that he is the author of lessons learned process and he also contributed to the creation of the phase-review process. The Case Company X had a lessons learned process for a long time, in the form of a *"lessons learned exercise"*, which was a requirement at the end of each project, and without it the project wouldn't be considered completed. During this exercise data were collected and discussed and an action plan was created. A written report was also prepared, which *"if they were lucky"* went to the database. Case Company X felt that this exercise procedure needed to be changed therefore a new lessons learned process was introduced. With the new process the objective was to set up a lessons learned review committee which would collect and filter the lessons learned received, and decide which ones are more relevant and can be changed into processes and procedures and/or in improvement projects wherein someone might take on and improve projects. The information received is enormous, therefore we ensure that we emphasize the issues which are considered to be useful but on which no action has been taken yet. Moreover, these lessons are published in the database for the project managers and other team members to use them. A specific website has been constructed solely for the lessons learned. The lessons learned are categorized in four broad categories: costs, people, process and procedures and technical. Moreover, there are sub-categories which are not finalized yet and are continuously updated. One particular idea was expert lessons transfer wherein *"they recommend the top five things you should do in a project"*. He feels this is important because rather than picking up the lessons for the last two-three years, you pick up experiences for the past twenty years of experienced project and programme managers.

Lessons learned are reviewed by a sub-committee, who decide upon the key lessons learned which should be submitted for a further review. Once decided, they are submitted to the (LLRC), who holds official meetings once in two months. The LLRC is in charge of filtering the information, retaining and publishing the necessary information and disposal of not applicable information. The LLRC have participants from all disciplines, which makes it more credible. The positive movement is the increased number of people interested to participate in the LLRC meetings. The LLRC makes the decisions if the lessons learned should change the process, improve the projects or no action to be taken. If there is a decision for a process change, it has its own procedure wherein the process owner needs to have the overall agreement on the change, and if changed, an email is sent for notification. There are no formal sessions or workshops organized for every process changed.

During the project the project group stops and reviews their work after every phase of the project, and they are subject to so-called *"phase reviews"* within Case Company X. This is made with the purpose of ensuring production of lessons learned for that particular phase as well as the review of the lessons learned from the previous phase(s). The written reports from the projects are submitted to the Quality department who then forwards them to the LLRC, who filters them every two months. Then, they are separated either under *"process change, improvement projects or data for storing"*. This is currently the process of lessons learned, and he considers it to be a step forward for Case Company X, always considering that there is always room for improvement and that nothing is perfect. He believes that the lessons learned process is a mechanism which will contribute positively to the project feedback, and certainly will not be the only one. He stated that it is newly compulsory (six months) to do the lessons learned report, and the way it is ensured that it is done is through the phase reviews. LLRC has had only three meetings so far, so it is a fairly new process. Considering that it is a fairly new process, the number of data which we received so far is small, considering that not many projects have completed their phases. Nevertheless, the measures to capture the data are established and are in place. He claims that the lessons learned are not compulsory for the project managers yet, and most of them have not routinely referenced the data from the past, because it was not part of the process.

He recognizes the need for a motivation scheme (i.e. especially monetary) but that has not been decided so far. He specifies the reward scheme based on performance for the project managers, but states that *"project managers are not rewarded if they make a change to the process or if they share a good thing they did with other people."* Therefore, this puts the project manager in the mindset of trying to finish the project on time, and minimize risk to his project. So even if they come up with something new, they do not have the actual time of passing it on to someone else. He states that *"the project manager is actually rewarded not to make change"*, which creates the paradox.

In smaller projects the PM will struggle, because there is no time or capital to work on the information to improve and change the processes. Project QA take the information and turn it into a process change, because they own the process, but we also deal with timescales etc. PM will tell you about things but not invest the time. *"We do it other way around, we incentive no change over change!"* he states. The other major problem which he perceives with companies like Case Company X is that the best people are far too busy in the midst of their deliveries even though they always get volunteered for improvement activities.

He argues that the phase review process is a very good process, and the projects that have a budget of 2-5 million are subject to phase reviews. Nevertheless, he states that in the last LLRC meeting, all the projects should be subject to mini-phase reviews which will be conducted by the quality assurance manager of the project. The process will be the same, but it will be conducted at a smaller scale with only project manager and quality assurance manager asking the phase review questions. The outcome will be reported at the local level in the project MRI. He feels that the phase reviews are important and they moved the projects on a positive note. The questions of the phase reviews have been a *"constantly growing series of questions"* and are general to all the projects. In his opinion, sometimes the questions are too close to the projects and sometimes they are too far away, so it goes both ways. In the training given for phase reviews, he specifies that the skilled people need to answer the questions posed by the phase reviews, and again the time constraint is the problem. He believes the biggest problem is *"locking up the skilled people to spend enough time on the phase reviews"*. He has uttered a wish to improve the answers to the phase review questions, and complete the checking exercise. The output of the phase reviews is used by the projects to fix the problem, but it is more at the local level, wherein the projects in 99% of the times fix the problem, but the way of fixing it is not transmitted to the wider audience. The output of the phase reviews at this time is *"individually held"*, and they are trying to make it available to a broader audience.

Regarding the database, he seems to be aware of different databases. He specifically emphasizes the fact that projects have their locally controlled databases, i.e. actions and decisions logs, which are locally managed. *"As an organization we haven't spent the time to review all the information managed at the local level in projects"* he says. A lesson learnt should be one database for everybody which is centralized and applicable for everyone. The specific site is a brand new site, and it hasn't been well tested enough to know if it is good or bad at this moment of time. There are actual statistics which show the number of people checking the database, and the usage has increased since its official publication. He feels there is a need to publicize the database to a wider audience in order to increase its usage, and it was encouraging to see the statistics increasing. They have ensured that people participating in the LLRC publicize the new database creation in their specific areas, we are doing local publicity. The publicity was done mostly through informal channels especially through the quality assurance teams, and the only formal method was the announcement on the main intranet site of the Case Company X.

On the question if as a result of phase reviews and lessons learned the processes are changed on a frequent basis, he replied that nothing is often enough; processes need to change all the time. Over the last three years all the processes have undergone a change cycle. He feels that especially for phase review procedures and closeout procedures which he looks after, every six months is not often enough to adopt a change, because as things go wrong you realize you need to add something in. A review cycle is done every two years, wherein all the processes are reviewed, wherein the process owner can confirm if he/she wants to change it or not. He feels that during his 4 years working history with Case Company X, the processes have not been changed enough and there has not been enough improvement. And he believes that the main reason for that is *"because the best people are doing something else"*.

The respondent feels that the commitment to follow the processes and procedures represents a problem, without consistency there is no improvement. *"We do not follow procedures as much as we'd like to"*. He feels happy if people challenge a procedure, and not just ignore it considering that something can be done to improve it. The reason behind it is the culture within the company, wherein he quotes his quote *"it's easy to do things wrong"* which is visible in the lessons learned website. The processes are there to do things only once and get it right, in the order given. Considering the pressures people have during their work, they decide to "take shortcuts" which creates problems and inconsistencies. It is easy to say that processes are complicated and difficult, but that is an easy excuse, and it is based on "*individual laziness*" and "*not making the time to follow and understand the processes*".

There are formal and informal ways of changing and updating the processes. He says that informal can be an email describing what is the problem with the process, and once the process is up for review the comments are taken into consideration. He feels that some individuals say that Case Company X is a procedure-oriented culture but on the other side are not aware of the details of the procedures, which is "*on the weird side*". People do things because they create "*an illusion of quality*" because they thing they are doing them for quality reasons. A culture with "lack of challenge" is dominant for the majority of people within Case Company X if he talks about generalization.

He suggests that Case Company X needs to provide an environment where junior employees can gain access to the bigger picture by having full visibility of a project- viewing all the available information, including documentation. This enables them to take ownership of project decisions. Also, the senior managers are freer to dedicate their time to the phase reviews and the lessons learned processes, and this ensures good results. Take the best people away from projects, because you need to invest in the future and if people can escape from day to day activities. If you don't have any type of project responsibilities for a period of time (six months or longer) to work on improvement activities rather than being stuck on fixing the same problems over and over again. Investment by the organization, something without a solution for the moment, because of the fact that high investment on important projects requires the best people to work on them. To put junior staff into senior positions followed by "*heavier mentoring*", to break out the cycle a little bit, and the senior person will be available.

Interview 5. Programme 4 – Executive Director – Board Member

Projects and programmes are managed at arm's length from the leadership of the organization and within the internal logic of the project management paradigm. He emphasized the difference of Case Company X if compared to other companies because it doesn't have external customers. The customers within Case Company X need to be created internally, and they are in charge of budget approval and/or any changes in scope. Moreover, he explains that changes are done through a mechanism within Case Company X called the project boards, which are important in terms of approving the scope, controlling the budget and preparing the organization for change.

The respondent categorizes the reviews into formal and independent reviews. In formal reviews, with the cycle of every six weeks, the PM(s) and the PgM(s) need to demonstrate that *"they have got their project under control"*. Based on the outcomes and results the projects are rated in red, amber and green. *"The review process is very structured"* he says. Also, there are independent reviews of projects, wherein a phase review is conducted at the end of each phase in the pre-defined project life cycle.

He states that the mixture of project boards, formal and independent reviews is vital for good and successful project management, and *"it's about how well you do them and not that you just have them"*. He emphasizes the importance of quality of the reviews, as well as the structural point of view. He elaborates more on his personal experience while attending the CPR(s), wherein he says that he would check three things *"quality, cost and on time delivery"*. Each process in the company is structured around these three things. During the review, a more in depth analysis is done for scheduling, critical path, cost optimization and risk, which he considers key parts of the project. These are done through specific processes which are fundamental processes in project management.

"I don't like sending people on training courses externally to share knowledge" he says. Even though it is done within Case Company X on occasional basis, he believes that the best way of sharing knowledge is on job training (OJT). Its all about getting them doing the job, and having their peers in the hierarchy teaching them how to do it. He feels that even though people can go to project management courses, learn and understand the theory, when they come back the theory is not applied which contributes to them forgetting it in a short period of time. Therefore, he thinks the practicing hands on project management is the best way to learn and share knowledge.

If a new tool, technique or process is about to be introduced, the company first develops pilot projects and tests it on a group of people internally first to ensure that it is functioning properly. This is done with the purpose of making sure that people are using it and understanding it. After, if there is no problem with the pilots, they are introduced to a wider audience, and institutionalized as a process/procedure and with the passage of time converted into the company's routine.

In terms of where Case Company X stands in project management, the vision is highlighted. There is a clear statement of intention, purpose and direction put in place which is understood throughout the company. Moreover, the engagement of stakeholders and people is present to build a collective capability for delivering the best results. In 2004, the Company has undergone a change and established a goal of being world class in the project management. Therefore, a project management capability maturity model was used which represents the road map for Case Company X. In 2004, it enabled the company to measure themselves and even though they believed that they were on level 3-4 out of 5 being highest, they have discovered they were on level 1.4. This result made them realize that they have a long and difficult journey in front of them. During these years the company has developed and improved in terms of processes and mechanism used in project management and this year they are aspiring to be on level 4. The fact that they have drastically moved forward in the short amount of time gives a boost to employees in Case Company X and makes people realize at any point how good they are.

"The key is to have a vision and make sure that people understand what the vision is" he says. Moreover, this can be understood only by utilizing the mechanisms and processes on a day-to-day basis. The vision of Case Company X was transmitted to people by launching a big event in 2004, and was illustrated with team exercises, wherein people were directly involved in the process. The update on changes and further successes is continuous in Case Company X, by organizing seminars and involving people. He considers people are an important asset to the company. He identified their need to be updated on where the Case Company X is in the road map illustrates and emphasizes the achievements as well as prepare them for what is coming next. *"Communication is very important"* he states.

Except on a strategic company level, communication is also important in a project itself. Most of the projects within Case Company X do not involve only technical change, but it involves people as well. Project management needs to focus on people issues as much as processes – to have success. Change management is of crucial importance and Case Company X makes attempts to understand and embrace the changes. Balance planning and emergence, and learning to work with ambiguity and uncertainty is crucial. Considering that it is change management process, much of time is developed and invested in good communication on project niches and communication plans. *"It's really a live thing and we really make sure we are communicating it properly from me as a board member downwards"* he explains. Effective communication is fundamental for Case Company X, so that a common understanding is gained.

Briefing sessions/meetings are organized on a weekly basis from the project community or from him to inform people on the critical issues which need to be discussed. Some of the issues are published on the intranet so that a wider audience is informed. The publication on the intranet depends on the importance and the criticality of the work done.

Considering that he is a member of the board, he explained that the management makes a commitment to the customers and to the board by setting the key milestones and doing the impossible to achieve them. The commitment is made at the beginning of each year, and the key milestones are specific to the year and are incorporated in the business plan. He goes into detail explaining that this year there are a total of 10 milestones. As the Programme Manager put it:

"We can't change it, it is set in stone and our board expects us to achieve them 10 out of 10, and also customers have the same expectation. We can't hide and change them, and make excuses. It is what it is and we have to do it, and this year we are going to achieve them. Our record was excellent in the past years; one exception was made this year where 23 out of 24 were achieved. Case Company X has a performance that you don't see often in companies. And...it's all about commitment, profiles, processes and mechanisms"

In regards to processes, Case Company X has a balance in changing them and making them better by optimizing them. With the increase of project management capability new processes are developed and introduced, and people are briefed on their usage. Nevertheless, *"I just worry we just change things for the sake of changing things without really analyzing if the particular change will give us a benefit"* he says. There have been conversations about project reviews processes, on how to proceed with them, and *"they have not convinced me they are doing it for the right reason, so they went away to have a look at it again"* he explains. One area where the Case Company X is working at the moment is the applicability of the current processes to all projects, because he feels that some of the processes are a little heavy for the smaller projects. The debate is still continuing on streamlining some of the processes, and the decision will be made in the near future.

The company is in stage 4 of the capability road map, which is all about getting the data and optimizing the data so that continuous improvement is achieved. There are new mechanisms being introduced, the latest being the *"critical chain"* which is a way of planning and controlling the project. He emphasizes that it is a quite advanced mechanism and there is a need to be able to plan really well to do it. The company wouldn't have been able to look at this mechanism two-three years ago because it would have meant to *"speak a common language"* which was not the case before. Nowadays, the company has reached that stage and can proceed safely to more advanced tools and mechanism, accompanied with streamlined processes. There is a joint desire to get real benefits from an integrated planning process to provide robust information to make timely and effective decisions in managing the projects.

Interview 6. Senior Programme Manager – Programme 5

The person has an Engineering background, and has been in Case Company X since 1991. He initially started working as a consultant and contractor before being officially hired by Case Company X and becoming a Project Manager which position he currently holds. He worked in the project environment all of his working life.

Under his supervision there are 40 staff based in two centers: X and Y. The current ongoing projects are a total of 8 in X, and 10 in Y. He explains that the current biggest projects are involved in the building of X Center, which is covering 80-90% of total expenditures of the programme. New X center is part of Case Company X's two center strategy, one based at X and one at Y. This major project will go into service officially in January 2010. When asked on the progress, the respondent replied that everything is going in accordance with the plan, and the allocation will be done in three different groups.

In terms of the PM(s) working under his jurisdiction, he thinks that technical skills are important, but in addition to other *"soft skills"* which he states that *"sometime are more important than technical skills"*. He argues that Case Company X has a fairly academic way of selecting personnel and measuring the project management capability in the organization. But, he feels that sometimes people will fall into jobs *"just for being at the right place at the right time"*. He also illustrates cases of senior engineers by default ending up in management positions. PM role is getting more generalized rather than specific as engineers.

At present, he states that Case Company X is matrix managed, so the only people under his supervision and 'control' are the PM(s) and the Project Planners (PPs). Other personnel in projects are allocated from the work centers, and they work simultaneously on the multiple projects. He feels that this contributes to knowledge sharing and transfer considering that they pick up on experience during the years and transmit it to their people. He does not think that the model of personnel being full time dedicated only to the one project is more productive; because the knowledge remains with them if/when they leave. With the current model utilized by Case Company X, he believes that the knowledge remains within the company. Nevertheless, he feels that in Case Company X there are some key individuals, which rarely do the same job twice. If they are good in their performance, they get promoted and move on, and the knowledge goes with them. In this particular case, they could serve as mentors to the more junior staff, so that they can absorb the knowledge first-hand.

When asked on the architecture establishment of Case Company X for knowledge transfer, he feels it not as good as he personally would like it to be. Especially he emphasized that sometimes even after 16 years of working experience with project management within Case Company X, he feels that the lessons are not always being learned. He uses the term *"reinvent the wheel"* wherein the same mistakes are being made, which makes him question the efficiency of the processes and the personnel. Nevertheless, he argues that it is not completely negative, considering that the processes are developed. *"The processes are perfect and contribute to knowledge transfer, but you get the human nature of it which prevents it from being as good as it could be"* he argues. In addition, he states that the processes are not that difficult to use. People get the right training on how to use the processes, and new processes launched are introduced to staff through sessions. But the feedback he gets from his staff is that they are many in terms of quantity. They are also heavy in terms of volume and of time consumption. Nevertheless, he feels that the standard and quality of the results of process usage depends on individual as well as divisions/departments knowledge. *"Anyone has the right to initiate a process change"* he says. He doesn't believe that people challenge the processes to the same level as they complain about them, for which he blames the human nature. Considering their tight schedule, they lack the time to invest in process change. Also, there is another overhead put on people to fill the form for a process change, and track its progress, and there is a bureaucracy behind it that impedes people from initiating a process change.

He finds that meetings are organized too often in Case Company X. There is a strong interdependence between programs and projects within programmes, and an update in one system, for example communication, impacts the other systems accordingly. He criticizes the fact that sometimes too many people get involved and everyone can find a reason to be present in a particular meeting. *"Sometimes people are in meetings because there is nothing else for them to do"* he explains. Currently, he thinks that the company is overstaffed and it reduces the efficiency in performance.

In regard to the lessons learned process he questions how many people actually comply with it to full extent, and complete lessons learned report for example. In addition, he questions the quality of the report, and what are the further actions, if any, undertaken.
He strongly believes that people do not use the lessons learned for their future and current projects. In his specific case, he encourages his PM(s) to review the lessons learned and incorporate them in the agenda of the monthly project reviews and in kick off meetings for the

starting projects. He feels that it should be a compulsory requirement for PM(s) to reference lessons learned in the project(s), and they need to disseminate it to their team members. Moreover, he thinks that there needs to be some kind of quantitative or qualitative evidence that the lessons learned, when and if produced, have been learnt and the same mistakes are not repeating. He recognizes the need to use the lessons learned database, but considering that it's a new database, he didn't have the chance to use it yet.

He recognized the benefit of the phase reviews and the CPRs for the company knowledge transfer and sharing. Nevertheless, he questions sometimes his personal benefit, considering that being a chairman of CPR takes time which he finds it difficult to find considering the workload. He asks *"what is in it for him personally"*. Also he questions if the right phase-review team is brought in to conduct the review. He finds that the more senior the person the more capable he/she is and the more stretched they are in terms of time. Therefore, it becomes a matter of overhead for people to be part of the phase and critical project reviews. He personally knows people that stopped being part of the reviews because of inability to allocate time to it.

Regarding the database, he says that it is reasonably ok, but it contains a lot of information, sometimes found not relevant for his personal need. It is a management system that collects everything, and has a detailed planning option. He feels that the management system is definitely a not user-friendly system, containing too much information. People need to be really trained to use it otherwise you cannot navigate with it. Everyone has the management system on their machine when they log on, and each person has different access capabilities, depending on their role in the project. He explains the situation:

"Unless you are really trained to use the management system, you cannot plan anymore. For example, I cannot go into management system and produce a simple, plan because I couldn't just do it. And training takes too long, so I lose the will to do it.....Before, when we used the Microsoft Project it was fairly easy...With the management system it is a big difference...not even the manual helps to operate it."

He recognizes the need for a motivation scheme, but he doesn't see it happening in the future. *"We would incentivise for performance delivery of individual projects, but not specifically to the knowledge sharing and transfer"* he states.

In terms of vision, Case Company X has improved significantly in the last 4-5 years. Nowadays, there is the road map – the capability maturity model- which he considers very crucial for the company. *"The implementation of projects is being done across all disciplines, and this was not the case just 5 years ago"* he explains. But, even though a common management reporting system is in place, he feels that still something is missing to reach full capability and maturity within Case Company X. He feels that Case Company X has become more results oriented in the last year or two. It has been part privatized for the past 7 years, which made them become more commercially aware and more commercially oriented. The company has been re-branded, and the image was changed which he considers a significant step forward. But with the change in image, he feels the way the projects are run and the way the results are produced didn't change significantly. He is aware of Case Company X applying the latest methodologies in project management, and their current priority is full application of the critical chain. He underlines that in other divisions like engineering and operations the road map journey is only on 1.4 while in the programme management it has reached 4, therefore, there is a need within other divisions to keep up with the project management capability achievements.

Positive and co-operative organizational culture is one of the main features of the company. Nevertheless, he does not see the culture in Case Company X as a no-blame culture at all. On the contrary, if people make mistakes, they are held accountable and responsible for their delivery. But if the model of the company changed to a much leaner organization, a no-blame culture could be more encouraged and embedded in the current structures. Regarding co-operation, they have developed a so-called *'program management stand'* wherein feedback and perception of personnel is given on project and programme managers. Specifically, they are evaluated in four categories: improvement, delivery, listening and performance. The current KPI set is 70% for all the categories, and at the moment the highest is in the delivery, which again confirms the result oriented culture.

SPM states that the main knowledge resource lies in people's heads. Nevertheless, all the employees are equipped with templates- tools which help them to articulate and record their activities, decisions and issues so that they can be re-used in different projects. The SPM interviewed underlined the fact that the presence of formal tools to capture knowledge contributed to the re-use of project knowledge. In the certain phases where knowledge does not become embedded in drawings or reports, he states that people rely on personal and informal contacts for knowledge transfer purposes.

He has uttered a wish that processes be streamlined to be able to apply them in projects of all sizes and scopes. He feels that some of the processes are too heavy and to detailed for the small projects.

Personal background

The person has an engineering background, and has been in Case Company X since 1979. He initially started working in the Engineering Center, and continued with software development, PMO Manager before becoming the Programme Specialist which position he currently holds.

He is part of the sub-programme called the Z, which is part of the major programme 6. The sub-programme started in 2001, and it is expected to end in 2012. The sub-programme has a sequence of projects and currently there are five projects running simultaneously, at different delivery stages. Currently the sub-programme is going through major rescheduling, and there were changes applied. His involvement with the sub-programme is recent. There are a total of 23 projects, and some of them are repetitive with lots of similarities. Therefore, they decided to group them in four groups. In addition, they decided to develop a generic vPMP and fPMP covering the governance section of the projects. He elaborates on the content of fPMP, which covers the static parts, and the vPMP which covers reporting. Reporting gives an idea on *"what do we expect to have done, what has to be done, and what are the changes"*.

Considering his long term experience with Case Company X, he claims that Case Company X is totally different from how it used to be; there have been major changes applied and it has improved for the better. He underlined the CMM road map, which provides a measure for them against the project management capability. He explains that at an initial stage of applying CMM, they have taken a snapshot and realized that they are only in the beginning of a long and difficult journey. But, with Case Company X continuously striving for improvement throughout the years; they have arrived at stage 4 out of 5. He feels that there have been major improvements'' as a result of CMM, the key one being *"standardization"*. *"It saves time and reinventing the wheel every time a project is executed"* he says.

Their programme has different feedback mechanisms which they utilize. There are staff briefings, which are organized on a weekly basis to provide quick updates of 15 minutes, with an agenda incorporating key issues. Moreover, there are monthly briefings at project and programme level which are more detailed and give more comprehensive presentations, with duration of two hours. All the PM(s) are required to report for their project(s). At the end of the meeting, they developed the practice of distributing a sheet so that everyone can write their thoughts on the meetings, and give suggestions for the future. These sheets are reviewed and changes are implemented accordingly. Staff communication is encouraged and measured with a KPI; which each programme area has to reach. KPI progress is updated on a monthly basis by the PMO manager.

Considering that his programme is part of top 20 Case Company X projects, the projects are part of CPR, which is conducted every 6-8 weeks. The report is submitted to the CPR, and he presented to the researcher the categorical organization, as well as the templates with detailed content. He specifies that the reports are checked upon submission by the PDFO. He says that there are internal reviews conducted within each project, organized on a monthly basis by the respective PM. In addition, internal reviews are conducted at programme level as well, on a monthly basis, and led by the SPM. At programme level, the PM(s), PMO manager and PP(s) need to be present.

Moreover, the projects are subject to phase reviews. He believes that the purpose of the phase review is to see if you have achieved the desired result, and if so, you are given permission to move to the next phase. In his projects, they apply a slightly different technique for phase reviews by taking a snapshot of a project at the current time, and focusing on only one specific important issue (i.e. risk, cost optimization) and detailing it. He finds the questions of the phase reviews not applicable to his projects, because the standard checklist given cannot be applied. The person in charge for phase reviews within his programme takes a pragmatic view of it, by choosing one key topic and detailing it, and producing a report with recommendations and improvements. At project level, there are also peer reviews conducted, at formal and informal levels. He feels that through involvement of other PM(s) the knowledge is transferred.

Lessons learned that are produced from previous projects are used and referenced in future radar projects. He emphasizes that his team conducts their own lessons learned where they try to capture what has been learnt from previous deliveries, and they are used for future estimates. This enables them to understand what actions teams undertook before in similar projects, and what mistakes, if any, did they make. But he argues that the usage and referencing of lessons learned in current and future projects is not compulsory within programme division in Case Company X.

The common management system is utilized for planning, manpower resources, ordering and it is totally integrated according to the interviewee. He feels it is not a user-friendly system, which feeling he had when it was first introduced, considering the system to be complicated and difficult. Nowadays, he is more familiar with the system and has developed shortcuts to get the desired outcome. The training provided by Case Company X for usage of management system was not good enough, and it was given a bit too late, he states. Nevertheless, the training has improved after considering the feedback of people, and they have also developed online self-guides which can be referenced. Regarding access, he argues that everyone has the level of access they need for their level of job.

In knowledge transfer, he emphasized the importance of domain expertise, which he illustrates with the example of supply chain management experts. They are experts in managing suppliers, and a person within the company who has never worked with suppliers can learn from them and ask for advice. In this way the experience of supply managers is absorbed and transmitted. At present, there is also a competence framework being developed by Case Company X, which will be implemented in the near future. The competence framework enables assessment of individual and division knowledge and identifies the need for training and further development.

He is also aware of the informal knowledge transfer within Case Company X. It is illustrated with the example of OJT, wherein project managers and other team members share their expertise and knowledge with a junior new person in the team. In their programme, they organize regular lunchtime sessions, wherein people usually volunteer to do a session on a key topic like communication and/or cost optimization. Moreover, there are away days organized across all programmes outside company premises, wherein discussions are conducted on important topics.

He specifies the initiative called Coaching for Performance, which has a sub-part called Career Development Opportunity Exchange (CDOX). This initiative enables people within Case Company X to relocate, enabling job rotation. They publish the available job opportunities and if people are interested to participate they can apply. This is valid only for staff internal to Case Company X, but across all divisions, not only programme division. The duration of stay in the new job to be tested can range from 1 day to six months, one year. It depends if the job is suitable to the requirements of the person. He strongly believes that way enables sharing and transmitting knowledge within the company. There are successions planning sessions organized, wherein a contingency plan is developed if someone leaves the job, so that he can be replaced.

When asked about processes and their effectiveness, the respondent replied that they are better than they used to be. He wasn't pleased with the fact that one set of processes are being applied to all projects, whether they are a multi-million pounds programme or a 20 thousand pounds project. *"With the best will of the world, this is not applicable in practice and it doesn't work"* he says. Even though the processes are improved and revisited more often than they used to be, especially since the CMM was put in place, he regards RAMP as a process which is a blocker for many people, considering the level of complicatedness and time consumption. He feels that there is a lot of time spent to put information in RAMP, instead of really understanding risk, which is what you are supposed to do actually. "It is difficult to fix it and make it say what you want it to say" he states.

The processes are not challenged as much as they should according to the interviewee. The possibility to change them and challenge them is there. At the end of each template there is a section for process improvement, which can be clicked and recommendation for change can be given. Even though he has used it himself in the past, he is not aware of many people actually using it. He believes the reason is the lack of time to actually track the progress of change, embedded in bureaucracy, as well as the lack of HR resources to investigate the processes and change them. He explains that each process has a process champion nominated, and for a change or update a key group of people needs to get involved to review it and sort it out before it gets published. Moreover, for new processes introduced, there are sessions held at different levels within the company depending on the degree of importance. The interviewee presented to the researcher the long list of the procedures and processes and templates which are in place, to which he expressed the impossibility to absorb all of them. He would have liked the processes to be streamlined and to be available to a lesser extent in terms of quantity. He praises the initiative of establishing a PDFO which is running a series of accelerating ATM projects, in order to improve and streamline the necessary processes.

The project staff is encouraged to become members of professional bodies such as APM, PMI and PMA. This is their way of contributing to communities of practice. Case Company X funds external training courses which are developed by APM for their employees.

APPENDIX B

The interview guide

Tacit Knowledge
- Reuse of tacit knowledge;
- Learning from projects;
- Tacit knowledge mechanisms;
- Knowledge transfer between projects;
- De-briefing methods;
- Spoken feedback from project members;
- PM approach to learning from experience.

Explicit Knowledge
- Documentation based de-briefing methods;
- Knowledge transfer between projects;
- Storing lessons learned;
- Database utilization;
- Explicit knowledge mechanisms;
- ICT tools;
- Individual knowledge vs. company knowledge; and
- Written feedback from project teams.

Processes
- Knowledge transfer and learning processes;
- Challenging processes;
- Contribution to knowledge management;
- Types of processes utilized;
- How to change processes;

Environment
- Managements intentions to knowledge and learning;
- Learning organization;
- Organizational learning;
- Type of environment promoted for knowledge and learning;
- Overall vision; and
- Individual knowledge and its transfer to company knowledge

1920062R0007

Printed in Great Britain
by Amazon.co.uk, Ltd.,
Marston Gate.